T0283532

Hanne Andreassen Hjelmås · Torunn Steinsland
Creators of KlompeLompe

SUMMER KNITTING
for Little Sweethearts

40 Nordic-Style Warm Weather Patterns
for Girls, Boys, and Babies

Photography by Hanne Andreassen Hjelmås

SCHIFFER
CRAFT
4880 Lower Valley Road • Atglen, PA 19310

All rights reserved. No part of this work may be reproduced or used in any form or by any means—graphic, electronic, or mechanical, including photocopying or information storage and retrieval systems—without written permission from the publisher.

The scanning, uploading, and distribution of this book or any part thereof via the Internet or any other means without the permission of the publisher is illegal and punishable by law. Please purchase only authorized editions and do not participate in or encourage the electronic piracy of copyrighted materials.

"Schiffer," "Schiffer Publishing, Ltd.," and the pen and inkwell logo are registered trademarks of Schiffer Publishing, Ltd.

Designed by Anne Vines
Cover design by Ashley Millhouse
Photography: Hanne Andreassen Hjelmås
Type set in Nimbus Sans

ISBN: 978-0-7643-6606-2
Printed in China

Published by Schiffer Publishing, Ltd.
4880 Lower Valley Road
Atglen, PA 19310
Phone: (610) 593-1777; Fax: (610) 593-2002
Email: Info@schifferbooks.com
Web: www.schifferbooks.com

For our complete selection of fine books on this and related subjects, please visit our website at www.schifferbooks.com. You may also write for a free catalog.

FSC
www.fsc.org
MIX
Paper from responsible sources
FSC® C167893

This edition copyright © 2023 by Schiffer Publishing, Ltd.

Translated from the Norwegian by Carol Huebescher Rhoades

Photography by Hanne Andreassen Hjelmås

Originally published as *KlompeLompes Sommerbarn* © 2018, J. M. Stenersens Forlag AS, Oslo. © 2018, Hanne Andreassen Hjelmås and Torunn Steinsland.

Library of Congress Control Number: 2022944209

Contents

Introduction	5
Olivia Summer Onesie	8
Kangaroo Pants	12
Tulla Skirt	17
David Sweater-Jacket	20
David Rompers	24
David Socks	28
David Cap	31
Butterfly Cardigan	32
Butterfly Cap	36
Butterfly Headband	41
Eivind Sweater-Jacket	44
Billie Cap	49
Billie Shorts	52
Pocket Dress	56

Spinnvill Hooded Jacket	60
Blueberry Girl's Summer Kerchief	64
Gurine Vest	68
Dinosaur Cardigan	74
Dinosaur Cap	80
Dinosaur Headband	84
Pocket Rompers	86
Lace Tights	92
Little Deer Bonnet	96
Tilda Dress-Leotard	100
Vaja Tunic	106
Henry Pullover	110
Crowberry Cap	114
Wing Cardigan	117
Theodor T-shirt	122

Kristoffer Shorts	126
Little Garter-Stitch Rompers	128
Tilda Summer Dress	136
Trixie Pixie Cap	140
Treasure Baby Blanket	146
Whirligig Cap	148
Crocheted Flower	150
David Doll Jacket	152
David Doll Rompers	154
Tulla Doll Skirt	156
Blueberry Girl's Doll Kerchief	160
Sewn KlompeLompe Flower	162
Lilly Baby Cap	165
Index	167
Acknowledgments	168

Introduction

In the back of your mind, maybe you think knitted garments are really only meant for winter. We'd like to show you once and for all that, to the contrary, they can be worn all year, and are perfectly wearable for summer.

It's important to remember that knitwear isn't what it used to be, when once upon a time all the options were wintery—like bulky, itchy sweaters we were forced to wear when we went out into the cold. Today, we wear knitted garments as everyday clothing as well as for parties, and their light silhouettes and comfortable yarns mean that they can also be worn during the summer. These days, we have finer versions of merino yarn and blends with cotton to make garments that aren't too warm and are never itchy.

Gradually during our work at KlompeLompe, we've developed a sense about practical garments, such as, for example, the David rompers, which you'll find on page 24. The child will be well dressed, but the garment is also comfortable and useful for an active child. This book is full of patterns for fine summer clothes, but remember that these garments can easily be worn during the rest of year by changing what is worn underneath. With wool leggings under the Olivia summer onesie, it's perfect for winter.

You'll find a variety of simple sweater-jackets and cardigans embellished with pattern knitting. If you're not quite sure what to knit, we recommend a sweater-jacket. They're quite durable and can be worn together with all types of dressier outfits.

The types of yarn and needle sizes vary, and we've knitted the simpler garments with larger size needles. A simple cap such as Trixie Pixie is knitted with US 4 (3.5 mm) needles and can be made in an evening. Such quick projects are fun and also wonderful when you want to make a gift.

We list the yarns that were used for the knits in the photographs, but because yarn companies change their lines, it's inevitable that some of the yarns may be discontinued. If you can't find the yarn noted, or if you have different preferences, simply use a similar weight and type of yarn.

A number of the garments go well together. Little sister can, for example, wear pocket rompers while big sister gets a pocket dress. We also allowed ourselves the pleasure of designing doll-size versions of some designs. They start on page 152. Now, for example, both little brother and his teddy can wear a David jacket.

It's so much fun to see all the photos of the KlompeLompe clothing that our earlier readers have posted on Instagram and social media. It will make us happy to see what you conjure up from these patterns!

Enjoy your knitting.

ABBREVIATIONS

as est	as established, that is, continue in pattern
BO	bind off (= British cast off)
CC	contrast color (pattern color)
cm	centimeter(s)
CO	cast on
dpn	double-pointed needle(s)
g	grams
k	knit
kf&b	knit into front and then back of same stitch = 1 stitch increased
k2tog	knit 2 together = right-leaning decrease; 1 stitch decreased
k3tog	knit 3 together = right-leaning decrease; 2 stitches decreased
k4tog	knit 4 together = right-leaning decrease; 3 stitches decreased
LLI	Left-Lifted Increase = knit into left side of stitch below stitch just worked
m	meter(s)
M1	Make 1 = lift strand between two stitches onto left needle and knit into back loop = 1 stitch increased; stitch is twisted
M1p	Make1 purl = lift strand between two stitches onto left needle an purl into back loop = 1 st increase; stitch is twisted
MC	main color (background color)
mm	millimeters
p	purl
pm	place marker
psso	pass slipped stitch over
rem	remain/remaining
rep	repeat(s)
rnd(s)	round(s)
RLI	Right-Lifted Increase = knit into right side of stitch below loop on needle = 1 stitch increased
RS	right side
sl	slip
sl m	slip marker
ssk	(sl 1 knitwise) 2 times, insert left needle into sts and knit together through back loops = left-leaning decrease; 1 stitch decreased
st(s)	stitch(es)
tbl	through back loop
WS	wrong side
wyb	with yarn held in back
wyf	with yarn held in front
yd(s)	yard(s)
yo	yarnover
* - * or ( )	repeat the sequence between asterisks or parentheses

Olivia Summer Onesie

Ready for the party in this sweet onesie knitted in a cotton blend yarn. Continue wearing it through the fall with leggings and a leotard underneath.

SIZES: 0-2 months (3, 6, 12, 18 months, 2, 4 years)

FINISHED MEASUREMENTS:

Chest: Approx. 17¾ (19½, 21¼, 22½, 23¼, 23½, 24¾) in [45 (49.5, 54, 57, 59, 59.5, 63) cm]

Total length: Approx. 12¾ (13¾, 14½, 16¼, 17, 17¾, 20½) in [32 (35, 37, 41, 43, 45, 52) cm]

YARN: Sandnes Garn Duo (fine merino wool) [CYCA #3 —DK, light worsted, 55% merino wool, 45% cotton, 126 yd (115 m) / 50 g]

YARN COLORS AND AMOUNTS:

Warm Brown 3543: 100 (150, 150, 150, 150, 200, 250) g

NEEDLES: US sizes 2.5 and 4 (3 and 3.5 mm): 16 in (40 cm) circulars and sets of 5 dpn; optional: 32 in (80 cm) circular for magic loop

NOTIONS: 3 (3, 3, 4, 4, 4, 4) buttons

GAUGE: 22 sts on larger size needles = 4 in (10 cm).

Adjust needle size to obtain correct gauge if necessary.

The onesie is worked back and forth on a circular.

BODY

With smaller size circular and color A, CO 93 (93, 99, 101, 103, 105, 107) sts, work back and forth in k1, p1 ribbing for 6 rows; the 1st row is on RS. On the 3rd row, make a buttonhole as follows: Work across until 5 st rem, BO 2 sts, work 3 sts in ribbing. On the next row, CO 2 new sts over the gap.

NOTE: Make a total of 3 (3, 3, 4, 4, 4, 4) buttonholes, spaced about 1½ in / 4 cm apart.

Change to larger size circular. Continue in ribbing throughout over the outermost 6 sts at each side (button/buttonhole bands) and work rem sts in between in stockinette. Work 4 rows. On the next row (RS), increase 20 sts evenly spaced across the stockinette section = 113 (113, 119, 121, 123, 125, 127) sts.

Sizes 2 (4) years only: Work 5 (7) rows in stockinette. Knit 1 row and, *at the same time,* increase 10 (20) sts evenly spaced across the stockinette section = 135 (147) sts.

All sizes: Work 2 rows in stockinette.

Next Row: Purl (+ ribbing on bands) and, *at the same time*, set aside sts to holders as follows:
21 (21, 22, 23, 23, 24, 26) sts for front;
18 (18, 18, 18, 19, 22, 24) sts for sleeve;
35 (35,39, 39, 39, 43, 47) sts for back;
18 (18, 18, 18, 19, 22, 24) sts for sleeve;
21 (21, 22, 23, 23, 24, 26) sts for front.

LEFT FRONT

Work 8 (10, 10, 12, 12, 14, 14) rows in stockinette and ribbing as est. Set sts aside.

BACK
Work 8 (10, 10, 12, 12, 14, 14) rows in stockinette and ribbing as est. Set sts aside.

RIGHT FRONT
Work 8 (10, 10, 12, 12, 14, 14) rows in stockinette and ribbing as est. Set sts aside.

Now join all the pieces. Beginning with left front, knit 1 row and CO 11 (16, 18, 18, 20, 20, 20) sts between each front and back for underarms = 99 (109, 119, 121, 125, 131, 139) sts total.

Next Row (WS): Work ribbing as est on the 6 sts at each side and purl rem sts.
Now work a total of 8 (8, 10, 10, 12, 12, 14 14) rows with ribbing on 6 sts at each side and stockinette on the two fronts but ribbing on underarm and back sts.

Return to working ribbing on 6 sts at each side and stockinette on rem sts in between.

Work 2 rows in stockinette.

Next Row (RS): Increase 31 sts evenly spaced across stockinette.

NOTE: When you come to the last 6 sts, place these sts on a separate needle, overlap them over the first 6 sts and work the two sets of sts together (joining 1st st of each needle together). The all-stockinette round now begins at the center of these 6 sts. Continue, working in the round = 124 (134, 144, 146, 150, 156, 164) sts.

Lengthen back with short rows: K72 (77, 82, 83, 85, 88, 92); turn, yo, p20. Turn, yo, k25. Turn, yo, p30. Turn, yo, k35. Turn, yo, p40. Turn, yo, and knit to end of rnd. When you come to a yarnover, work yarnover and next st tog.

Continue around in stockinette until piece measures 11½ (12¼, 13, 14½, 15½, 16¼, 18½) in [29 (31, 33, 37, 39, 41, 47) cm] down center front.

Pm on each side of the 8 sts at center front and back. Increase with M1 on each side of the 8 sts = 4 sts increased. Increase the same way on every other rnd a total of 4 times. On next rnd, BO the center 8 sts of front and back and work each leg separately.

LEGS (make both alike)
With larger size dpn or magic loop circular, work the 62 (67, 72, 73, 75, 78, 82) sts around leg as follows: k11 (12, 14, 13, 14, 17, 17), *k2tog*; rep * to * 20 (21, 22, 23, 23, 22, 24) times, k11 (13, 14, 14, 15, 17, 17).

Change to smaller size needle and work 4 rnds k1, p1 ribbing. BO in ribbing on last rnd.

WINGS (same on each armhole)
With smaller size needles, begin on RS with held sts.
Purl 2 rows.

Wing Row 1 (RS): K6 (6, 6, 6, 6, 8, 9), M1, k2, M1, k2, M1, k2, M1, k5 (5, 5, 5, 6, 7, 8), 1 st rem; turn.

Wing Row 2: Sl 1, purl until 1 st rem; turn.

Wing Row 3: Sl 1, knit until 2 sts rem; turn.

Wing Row 4: Sl 1, purl until 2 sts rem; turn.

Wing Row 5: Sl 1, k4 (4, 4, 4, 6, 6, 7), M1, k2, M1, k2, M1, k2, M1, k5 (5, 5, 5, 6, 7, 8); turn.

Wing Row 6: Sl 1, purl until 3 sts rem; turn.

Wing Row 7: Sl 1, knit to end of row; turn.

Wing Row 8 (WS): Knit to end of row.

Wing Row 9 (RS): Change to larger size needles and BO knitwise.

With smaller size needle, pick up and knit sts from underside of wing on WS: 1 st in each st + 1 st on each side = 20 (20, 20, 20, 21, 24, 26) sts total.

Knit 1 row and then purl 1 row.

Next Row: K4 (4, 4, 4, 4, 6, 7), M1, *k2, M1*; rep * to * until 4 (4, 4, 4, 5, 6, 7) sts rem, k3 (3, 3, 3, 4, 5, 6); turn.

Next Row: Sl 1, purl until 1 st rem; turn.

Next Row: Sl 1, k5 (5, 5, 5, 6, 7, 9), M1, k2, M1, k2, M1, k4, M1, k2, M1, k2, M1, knit to end of row.

Knit 1 row.
With larger size needles, BO knitwise.

FINISHING
Weave in all ends neatly on WS. Sew on buttons. Block by covering onesie with a damp towel; leave until completely dry.

Kangaroo Pants

Quick-to-knit pants on larger-size needles,
great for a newborn up to a four-year-old.

SIZES: 0-2 months (3, 6 months, 1, 2, 4 years)

FINISHED MEASUREMENTS:

Chest: Approx. 17½ (19¾, 21, 23¼, 24¾, 26) in [44.5 (50, 53.5, 59, 63, 66) cm]

Total length: Approx. 13¾ (14½, 15¾, 17¼, 19¼, 22) in [35 (37, 40, 44, 49, 56) cm]

YARN: Sandnes Garn KlompeLompe merinoull [CYCA #3—DK, light worsted, 100% merino wool, 114 yd (104 m) / 50 g]

YARN COLORS AND AMOUNTS:

MC: Dark Gray-Blue 6061: 100 (150, 150, 200, 200, 250) g

CC: Light Petroleum Blue 6521: 50 g or leftovers

NEEDLES: US size 2.5 (3 mm): 16 and 32 in (40 and 80 cm) circulars—32 in (80 cm) for magic loop—and set of 5 dpn

US size 4 (3.5 mm): 16 or 24 in (40 or 60 cm) circular

GAUGE: 22 sts on larger size needles = 4 in (10 cm).

Adjust needle size to obtain correct gauge if necessary.

The garment begins at the back with the bib which is worked double. It is worked back and forth on a circular needle.

BIB

With smaller size circular and MC, CO 28 (32, 36, 40, 42, 44) sts, work back and forth in stockinette for 2½ (2¾, 3¼, 3½, 3½, 4) in [6 (7, 8, 9, 9, 10) cm]. Knit the next, WS, row for foldline. Work in stockinette for 2½ (2¾, 3¼, 3½, 3½, 4) in [6 (7, 8, 9, 9, 10) cm].

Place sts on a holder, fold piece and seam sides.

DOUBLE STRAPS

Right strap: With RS facing, on folded edges, pick up and knit 6 sts at top of bib and CO 6 sts = 12 sts. Now work around on dpn or with magic loop for 3½ (4, 4, 4¼, 4¾, 5¼) in [9 (10, 10, 11, 12, 13) cm].

On the next row, increase toward neck:
K1, M1, knit until 1 st rem, M1, k1. Continue in stockinette, increasing the same way on every other round until you have 28 (32, 36, 40, 42, 44) sts.

Place the first 14 (16, 18, 20, 21, 22) sts on one needle and the next 14 (16, 18, 20, 21, 22) sts on another needle. Using a dpn, join the two sets of sts, knitting tog the first st on each needle = 14 (16, 18, 20, 21, 22) sts rem. Leave the sts on dpn or holder.

Left strap: With RS facing, CO 6 sts and then pick up and knit 6 sts on left side of bib = 12 sts. Work as for right strap. When you've completed the increases, k14 (16, 18, 20, 21, 22) before you join the 2 sets of sts together.

Change to larger size needle and join the pieces as follows:

Beginning on right side, knit the right strap sts, CO 21 (23, 23, 25, 27, 29) sts, knit bib sts, CO 21 (23, 23, 25, 27, 29) sts, knit sts of left strap. Work in the round = 98 (110, 118, 130, 138, 146) sts.

Now work 6 rnds, knitting all sts except for the 21 (23, 23, 25, 27, 29) sts on each underarm which are worked in k1, p1 ribbing.

Raise back with short rows as follows:
K10; turn, yo, p20. Turn, yo, k25. Turn, yo, k30. Turn, yo, k35. Turn, yo, p40. Turn, yo, k20 (= to end of rnd. When you come to a yarnover, work yarnover and next st tog.

On the next rnd, make an opening for the pocket:
K39 (44, 48, 52, 56, 59), place 20 (22, 22, 26, 26, 28) sts on a holder, CO 20 (22, 22, 26, 26, 28) sts, k39 (44, 48, 52, 56, 59). Knit 1 rnd.

On next rnd, k39 (44, 48, 52, 56, 59), p20 (22, 22, 26, 26, 28), k39 (44, 48, 52, 56, 59).

Continue in stockinette until piece measures 11¾ (12¾, 13½, 15, 16½, 19¼) in [30 (32, 34, 38, 42, 49) cm] from shoulder.

Pm on each side of the center 6 sts on front and back. Increase with M1 on each side of these 6 sts on every other rnd a total of 4 times = 114 (126, 134, 146, 154, 162) sts.

On next rnd, BO the center 6 sts on front and back and work each leg separately = 51 (57, 61, 67, 71, 75) sts.

Work around in stockinette for ⅜ (⅜, ¾, ¾, 1¼, 1½) in [1 (1, 2, 2, 3, 4) cm]. Change to smaller size dpn.

Knit 4 rnds, purl 1 rnd, knit 4 rnds, binding off on last rnd. If you want a contrast color for the lower part of leg, change to CC on the 4th knit rnd = knit 1 rnd, purl 1 rnd, knit 4 rnds.

POCKET LINING
Change to CC. Work held sts on RS. Work 14 (16, 16, 18, 20, 22) rows in stockinette.
On next row (RS), decrease as follows:
K1, sl 1, k1, psso, knit until 3 sts rem k2tog, k1.
Purl 1 row.
Knit 1 row, decreasing as above, and, *at the same time*, BO knitwise.

FINISHING
With MC, sew pocket lining to back of pocket.
Fold each leg at foldline and sew down facing on WS.
Sew cast-on edge of bib to backside.
Weave in all ends neatly on WS.
Block by covering pants with a damp towel; leave until completely dry.

KlompeLompe merinoull, colors 2652 and 7251

KlompeLompe merinoull, colors 6521 and 1020

Tulla Skirt

A girl's favorite skirt with our well-known *tulla* texture pattern.

SIZES: 2 (4, 6, 8, 10-12) years

FINISHED MEASUREMENTS:

Waist: Approx. 19¾ (21, 21¾, 23¼, 24¾) in [50 (53, 55.5, 59, 63) cm]

Total length: Approx. 10¼ (11, 11¾, 12¾, 13¾) in [26 (28, 30, 32, 35) cm]

YARN: Sandnes Garn KlompeLompe Tynn merinoull (fine merino wool) [CYCA #1—fingering, 100% merino wool, 191 yd (175 m) / 50 g]

YARN COLORS AND AMOUNTS:

Powder Rose 4032: 150 (150, 150, 150, 200) g

NEEDLES: US size 2.5 (3 mm): 16 and 24 in (40 and 60 cm) circulars

NOTIONS: Waistband elastic—to fit around waist + seam allowance

GAUGE: 27 sts = 4 in (10 cm).

Adjust needle size to obtain correct gauge if necessary.

STITCHES AND TECHNIQUES

Elongated knit stitch (ek): knit 1 between the k2tog and 1 slipped st 2 rounds below, k1, pulling loop up with right needle tip to elongate it. Work the next ek in same hole. See video at klompelompe.no.

The skirt is worked bottom up, in the round on a circular needle.

SKIRT

CO 240 (240, 248, 264, 272) sts. Join, being careful not to twist cast-on row; pm for beginning of rnd.

Work 6 rnds in seed st (Rnd 1 = k1, p1; on subsequent rnds, work purl over knit and knit over purl). Knit 2 rnds.

TULLA PATTERN

Rnd 1: *K2tog, sl 1, k1, psso, k4*; rep * to * around.
Rnd 2: Knit around.
Rnd 3: *1 ek, k2, 1 ek, 4*; rep * to * around.
Rnd 4: Knit around.
Rnd 5: *K4, k2tog, sl 1, k1, psso*; rep * to * around.
Rnd 6: Knit around.
Rnd 7: *K4, 1 ek, k2, 1 ek*; rep * to * around.
Rnd 8: Knit around.

Repeat Rnds 1-8 of pattern until skirt measures approx. 4¾ (5½, 6¼, 7, 8) in [12 (14, 16, 18, 20) cm].
Knit 2 rnds, purl 1 rnd.
Decrease Rnd 1: *K6, k2tog*; rep * to * around = 210 (210, 217, 231, 238) sts rem.

Continue around in stockinette until skirt measures 6¾ (7½, 8¼, 9, 10¼) in [17 (19, 21, 23, 26) cm].

Decrease Rnd 2: *K5, k2tog*; rep * to * around = 180 (180, 186, 198, 204) sts rem.

Work around in stockinette for 1½ in (4 cm).

Decrease Rnd 3: *K4, k2tog*; rep * to * around = 150 (150, 155, 165, 170) sts rem.

Decrease Rnd 4: Knit, decreasing 14 (6, 5, 5, 0) sts evenly spaced around.

Work in seed st for 1¾ in (4.5 cm). Purl 1 rnd (foldline) and then work in stockinette for 1¾ in (4.5 cm). BO, making sure bind-off is not too tight.

FINISHING

Fold waist facing to WS and sew down, leaving an opening for elastic. Insert elastic and seam short ends of elastic; finish closing casing. Weave in all ends neatly on WS. Block by gently steam-pressing skirt under a damp pressing cloth.

David Sweater-Jacket →→

David Sweater-Jacket

A very wearable sweater with a rounded yoke and a simple textured stripe pattern. It's perfect to be passed down through the years from sibling to sibling.

SIZES: 0-1 (3, 6, 12, 18 months, 2, 4, 6, 8, 10 years)

FINISHED MEASUREMENTS:

Chest: Approx. 17¾ (20, 21½, 22, 24½, 24¾, 25½, 26, 28, 29¼) in [45 (51, 54.5, 56, 62, 63, 65, 66, 71, 74.5) cm]

Total length: Approx. 8¾ (9½, 10¼, 11, 12, 13½, 15¼, 17, 18½, 20) in [22 (24, 26, 28, 30.5, 34.5, 38.5, 43, 47, 51) cm]

YARN: Sandnes Garn KlompeLompe Tynn merinoull (fine merino wool) [CYCA #1–fingering, 100% merino wool, 191 yd (175 m) / 50 g]

YARN COLORS AND AMOUNTS:

Petroleum 7572: 100 (100, 100, 150, 150, 150, 200, 250, 250, 300) g

NEEDLES: US sizes 1.5 and 2. 5 (2.5 and 3 mm): 16 or 24 in (40 or 60 cm) circulars (or magic loop), sets of 5 dpn

NOTIONS: 5 (5, 6, 6, 7, 7, 8, 8, 8, 9) buttons

GAUGE: 27 sts on larger size needles = 4 in (10 cm).

Adjust needle size to obtain correct gauge if necessary.

The sweater is worked from the top down, back and forth on a circular needle.

With smaller size circular, CO 73 (75, 81, 85, 89, 93, 99, 103, 103, 107) sts. Work back and forth in k1, p1 ribbing for 6 (6, 6, 6, 8, 8, 8, 10, 10, 10) rows, **but**, on the 3rd row, make a

buttonhole: Work 3 sts ribbing, BO 2 sts, rib to end of row. On next row, CO 2 sts over gap. On the buttonhole band, make a total of 5 (5, 6, 6, 7, 7, 8, 8, 8, 9) buttonholes evenly spaced about 1¾ (2, 1¾, 1¾, 1¾, 2, 1¾, 2¼, 2½, 2¼) in [4.5 (5, 4.5, 4.5, 4.5, 5, 4.5, 5.5, 6, 5.5) cm] apart.

NOTE: From this point on, the outermost 5 sts on each side are always knitted on every row for the buttonhole/button bands. *Don't forget to make the buttonholes!*

Change to larger size circular. Knit 1 row, increasing 35 sts evenly spaced across, excluding bands = 108 (110, 116, 120, 124, 128, 134, 138, 138, 142) sts.

Work 4 rows in stockinette.

Knit 3 rows (= knit on WS, knit on RS, knit on WS).
Work 2 rows in stockinette (= knit on RS, purl on WS).
Next Row (RS): Knit 1 row, increasing 20 sts evenly spaced across, excluding bands = 128 (130, 136, 140, 144, 148, 154, 158, 158, 162) sts.
Work 4 rows in stockinette.

Knit 3 rows (= knit on WS, knit on RS, knit on WS).
Work 2 rows in stockinette (= knit on RS, purl on WS).
Next Row (RS): Knit 1 row, increasing 27 sts evenly spaced across = 155 (157, 163, 167, 171, 175, 181, 185, 185, 189) sts.

Work 4 rows in stockinette.

Knit 3 rows (= knit on WS, knit on RS, knit on WS).
Work 2 rows in stockinette (= knit on RS, purl on WS).
Next Row (RS): Knit 1 row, increasing 39 sts evenly spaced across, excluding bands = 194 (196, 202, 206, 210, 214, 220, 224, 224, 228) sts.
Work 1 (1, 4, 4, 4, 4, 4, 4, 4, 4) rows in stockinette.

Sizes – (–, 6, 12, 18 months, 2, 4, 6, 8, 10 years) only:
Knit 3 rows (= knit on WS, knit on RS, knit on WS).
Work 2 rows in stockinette (= knit on RS, purl on WS).
Next Row (RS): Knit 1 row, increasing 39 sts evenly spaced across, excluding bands = – (–, 241, 245, 249, 253, 259, 263, 263, 267) sts.
Work 0 (0, 1, 3, 1, 4, 4, 4, 4, 4) rows in stockinette.

Sizes – (–, –, –, – months, 2, 4, 6, 8, 10 years) only:
Knit 3 rows (= knit on WS, knit on RS, knit on WS).
Work 2 rows in stockinette (= knit on RS, purl on WS).
Next Row (RS): Knit 1 row, increasing – (–, –, –, –, 25, 30, 30, 50, 39) sts sts evenly spaced across, excluding bands = – (–, –, –, –, 278, 289, 293, 313, 306) sts.

Work 0 (0, 0, 0, 0, 1, 1, 3, 3, 4) rows in stockinette.

Size 10 years only:
Knit 3 rows (= knit on WS, knit on RS, knit on WS).
Work 2 rows in stockinette (= knit on RS, purl on WS).
Next Row (RS): Knit 1 row, increasing 21 sts evenly spaced across, excluding bands = 327 sts.
Work 0 (0, 0, 0, 0, 0, 0, 0, 0, 1) row in stockinette.

Sizes 3 and 18 months only:
Next Row (RS): Knit 1 row, increasing 27 (24) sts evenly spaced across, excluding bands = 223 (273) sts.
Work 1 row in stockinette.

All sizes:
You should now have 194 (223, 241, 245, 273, 278, 289, 293, 313, 327) sts.

On next row, divide for body and sleeves:
K29 (32, 35, 36, 39, 40, 41, 42, 45, 48), place 41 (48, 52, 52, 58, 58, 62, 62, 66, 68) sts on a holder for sleeve, CO 5 new sts for underarm, k54 (63, 67, 69, 79, 82, 83, 85, 91, 95), place 41 (48, 52, 52, 58, 58, 62, 62, 66, 68) sts on a holder for sleeve, CO 5 new sts for underarm, k29 (32, 35, 36, 39, 40, 41, 42, 45, 48).

Work 2 (0, 2, 0, 0, 2, 2, 0, 0, 2) rows in stockinette.

Continue textured stripe pattern:
Knit 3 rows (= knit on WS, knit on RS, knit on WS).
Work 7 rows in stockinette (= knit on RS, purl on WS).
Rep these 10 rows until body measures 8 (8¾, 9½, 10¼, 11, 12¾, 14¼, 15¾, 17¼, 19) in [20 (22, 24, 26, 28, 32, 36, 40, 44, 48) cm]

Change to smaller size circular and work 8 (8, 8, 8, 10, 10, 10, 12, 12, 12) rows in k1, p1 ribbing. BO in ribbing on last row.

SLEEVES (make both alike)
With larger size dpn, beginning in center st of the 5 sts cast-on for underarm, pick up and knit 3 sts, k41 (48, 52, 52, 58, 58, 62, 62, 66, 68) held sleeve sts, pick up and knit 2 sts on underarm.

TIP:

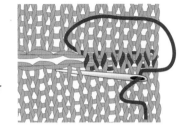

Kitchener stitch

If you have trouble picking up and knitting stitches, you can cast on new sts and later join them with Kitchener stitch.

Join to work in the round. The first st is a marked st (pm around st) and always purled.
Knit 2 (0, 2, 0, 0, 2, 2, 0, 0, 2) rnds.

Now work around in textured stripe pattern: Purl 1 rnd, knit 1 rnd, purl 1 rnd, knit 7 rnds.
Rep these 10 rnds for sleeve.

After ¾ in (2 cm), decrease 1 st on each side of marked st. Decrease the same way every 1 (¾, ¾, 1, ¾, 1, 1, 1¼, 1¼, ¼) in [2.5 (2, 2, 2.5, 2, 2.5, 2.5, 3, 3, 3) cm] until 38 (41, 41, 43, 43, 45, 47, 49, 51, 51) sts rem. Continue without further shaping until sleeve is 4¾ (5½, 6¼, 7, 8, 9, 10¼, 11½, 13, 14¼) in [12 (14, 16, 18, 20, 23, 26, 29, 33, 36) cm] long.
Knit 1 rnd, and, except on smallest size, decrease to eliminate marked st.
Change to smaller size dpn and work 8 (8, 8, 8, 10, 10, 10, 12, 12, 12) rnds in k1, p1 ribbing. BO in ribbing on last rnd.

FINISHING
Seam underarms. Sew on buttons. Weave in all ends neatly on WS.
Block by covering sweater with a damp towel and leaving it until completely dry.

Klompelompe
Brown color 2652 and
Blue-Petroleum color 7251

David Rompers

Complete the David set by making rompers in the same style.

SIZES: 0-2 (3, 6, 12, 18, 24, 36) months

FINISHED MEASUREMENTS:

Chest: Approx. 16½ (17½, 19, 19½, 20½, 21, 21¾) in [42 (44.5, 48.5, 49.5, 52, 53, 55.5) cm]

Total length, from bib down: pprox. 11¾ (13, 13¾, 15, 16¼, 17, 17¼) in [30 (33, 35, 38, 41, 43, 44) cm]

YARN: Sandnes Garn KlompeLompe Tynn merinoull (fine merino wool) [CYCA #1—fingering, 100% merino wool, 191 yd (175 m) / 50 g]

YARN COLORS AND AMOUNTS:

Brown 2652: 100 (100, 100, 100, 100, 100, 150) g

NEEDLES: US sizes 1.5 and 2. 5 (2.5 and 3 mm): 16 in (40 cm) circulars (or magic loop in smaller size), sets of 5 dpn in smaller size

NOTIONS: 2 buttons

GAUGE: 27 sts on larger size needles = 4 in (10 cm).

Adjust needle size to obtain correct gauge if necessary.

The rompers begin with the bib at the top and the garment is initially worked back and forth.

With smaller size circular, CO 37 (37, 39, 41, 43, 45, 47) sts. Beginning on RS, work 6 rows in k1, p1 ribbing, but, on 3rd row, make 2 buttonholes: 3 sts ribbing, BO 2 sts, continue in ribbing until 5 sts rem, BO 2 sts, work 3 sts in ribbing. On next row, CO 2 sts over each gap.

Change to larger size circular. Now work the outermost 4 sts at each side in garter st (= knit on all rows), and rem sts in 10-row textured stripe pattern = 7 rows stockinette, knit 1 row on WS, knit 1 row on RS, knit 1 row on WS.

Work in pattern as est until piece measures 3 (3¼, 3½, 4, 4, 4¼, 4¼) in [7.5 (8.5, 9, 10, 10, 11, 11) cm]. Cut yarn.

CO 39 (42, 46, 47, 49, 50, 52) sts, work the 37 (37, 39, 41, 43, 45, 47) sts already on needle as est, CO 38 (41, 45, 46, 48, 49, 51) sts = 114 (120, 130, 134, 140, 144, 150) sts. The first st is at center back – join and pm for beginning of rnd.

Now work 6 rnds in ribbing on the new sts you cast on + the 4 previously worked garter sts at each side. Rem sts are worked in textured stripe pattern.

Raise back with short rows as follows:
K10; turn, yo, p31. Turn, yo, k39. Turn, yo, p47. Turn, yo. Continue, working 8 more sts on each side every time you turn until you've turned a total of 3 (3, 3, 4, 4, 4, 4) times on each side. When you come to a yarnover, work yarnover and next st tog.
Continue, working in textured stripe pattern on all sts around and in row sequence on bib.

TEXTURED STRIPE PATTERN IN THE ROUND:
Knit 7 rnds, purl 1 rnd, knit 1 rnd, purl 1 rnd.

When piece measures 9½ (10¾, 11½, 12¼, 13, 13¾, 14½) in [24 (27, 29, 31, 33, 35, 37) cm], cut yarn and slip next 26 (28, 30, 31, 32, 33, 35) sts to right needle.
Work the back 50 (54, 58, 60, 62, 64, 68) sts (back) back and forth in textured stripe pattern.
On next RS row, k2tog, work until 2 sts rem, k2tog.
Decrease the same way on every RS row until 20 (20, 22, 22, 24, 24, 24) sts rem.

Place the 19 (20, 21, 21, 23, 23, 23) sts at each side onto holders and work the 26 (26, 30, 32, 32, 34, 36) sts at center front in textured stripe pattern. On next RS row, k2tog, work until 2 sts rem, k2tog. Decrease the same way on every RS row until 20 (20, 22, 22, 24, 24, 24) sts rem.

Continue in pattern without decreasing until front is approx. ¾ in (2 cm) shorter than back. BO. Join front and back with Kitchener st (see page 22).

With smaller size dpn, pick up and knit about 3 sts for every 4 sts around one leg, knit sts from holder. Divide sts onto 4 dpn and join.

Work 6 (6, 6, 8, 8, 8, 8) rnds in k1, p1 ribbing, binding off in ribbing on last rnd.

STRAPS
With smaller size needle, pick up and knit 19 sts at center back on ribbing. Work 10 (10, 10, 12, 12, 14, 14) rows in k1, p1 ribbing. On next row, BO center st and work each 9-st strap separately.

Work in k1, p1 ribbing until strap measures 6 (7, 8, 8¾ 9½, 10¼, 11) in [15 (18, 20, 22, 24, 26, 28) cm] from row where you picked up sts. BO and work second strap the same way.

FINISHING
Weave in all ends neatly on WS.
Sew on a button at end of each strap.
Block by covering rompers with a damp towel and leaving garment until completely dry.

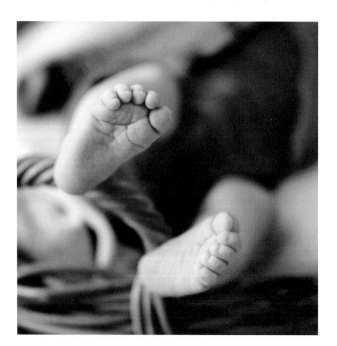

David Sweater-Jacket and
David Cap:
KlompeLompe Tynn
merinoull, Blue-Petroleum
color 7251

David Rompers:
KlompeLompe Tynn merinoull, Blue color 6033

David Socks

Easy socks that will fit baby perfectly.
The tie cords will keep them in place.

SIZES: 0-4 (4-12, 18 months, 2-3 years)

YARN: Sandnes Garn KlompeLompe Tynn merinoull (fine merino wool) [CYCA #1—fingering, 100% merino wool, 191 yd (175 m) / 50 g]

YARN COLORS AND AMOUNTS:
Brown 2652 (MC): 50 (50, 50, 50) g

NEEDLES: US size 2.5 (3 mm): set of 5 dpn or use 32 in (80 cm) circular for magic loop (see video on magic loop technique on KlompeLompe.no).

NOTIONS: length of thin cord to fit around ankle of each sock + enough extra for large bow and knot at each end

GAUGE: 27 sts = 4 in (10 cm).

Adjust needle size to obtain correct gauge if necessary.

The socks are knitted in the round from the cuff down.

CO 40 (42, 46, 48) sts. Divide sts onto dpn and join.
Purl 1 rnd, knit 1 rnd, purl 1 rnd, knit 7 rnds.
Rep * to * a total of 3 (4, 4, 4) times.

EYELET RND:
Size 0-4 months: (K2tog, yo, k2) around.
Size 4-12 months: (K2tog, yo, k2) 5 times, k2, (k2tog, yo, k2) 5 times.
Size 18 months: (K2tog, yo, k2) 5 times, k6, (k2tog, yo, k2)

5 times.
Size 2-3 years: (K2tog, yo, k2) around.

Knit 3 rnds. Cut yarn.
Place the first 12 (13, 14, 14) sts and last 12 (13, 14, 14) sts on a holder and work the center 16 (16, 18, 20) sts separately.

FRONT/INSTEP
Work back and forth in stockinette.
Work in stockinette for approx. 1⅜ (1¾, 2¼, 2½) in [3.5 (4.5, 5.5, 6.5) cm]
Next Row: K2tog, knit until 2 sts rem, sl 1, k1, psso.
Decrease the same way on every RS row a total of 3 (3, 4, 4) times and then BO on next, WS, row.

Begin again at center back where the round had begun previously.
Knit first set of sts from the holder, pick up and knit 3 sts for every 4 rows across instep and then knit rem sts on holder = 62 (68, 74, 80) sts. Divide sts onto dpn and work around in garter st (= alternate knit and purl rnds).

Work in garter st for 3.5 (3.5, 4.5, 5.5) ridges (2 rnds/rows = 1 ridge); the next row is knit.
Decrease as follows:
Decrease Rnd 1: K1, k2tog, k22 (25, 28, 31), k2tog, k8, k2tog, k22 (25, 28, 31), k2tog, k1.
Purl 1 rnd.

Decrease Rnd 2: K1, k2tog, k18 (21, 24, 27), k2tog, k2tog, k8, k2tog, k2tog, k18 (21, 24, 27), k2tog, k1.
Purl 1 rnd.

Decrease Rnd 3: K1, k2tog, k2tog, k17 (20, 23, 26), k2tog, k1, k2tog, k1, k2tog, k17 (20, 23, 26), k2tog, k2tog, k1.
Purl 1 rnd.

Decrease Rnd 4: K1, k2tog, k16 (19, 22, 25), k2tog, k3, k2tog, k16 (19, 22, 25), k2tog, k1.
Purl 1 rnd.

BO knitwise.

Seam sole of sock. Weave in all ends neatly on WS. Thread cord through eyelet rnd on sock.

Make second sock the same way. Place damp towel on socks and leave until completely dry.

David Cap

A cap knitted on small needles with the same textured stripe pattern as the rest of the garments in the David series. Embellish the cap with a fake fur pom-pom or make a pom-pom with leftover yarn.

SIZES: 0-1 (1-3, 3-6 months, 1, 2-3, 5-7, 8-10 years)

YARN: Sandnes Garn KlompeLompe Tynn merinoull (fine merino wool) [CYCA #1—fingering, 100% merino wool, 191 yd (175 m) / 50 g]

YARN COLORS AND AMOUNTS:

Gray-Blue 6571: 50 (50, 50, 50, 50, 50, 50) g

NEEDLES: US sizes 1.5 and 2.5 (2.5 and 3 mm): 16 in (40 cm) circulars and, in larger size, set of 5 dpn or use 32 in (80 cm) circular for magic loop (see video on magic loop technique on KlompeLompe.no).

NOTIONS: small fake fur pompom or make one with wool yarn remnants

GAUGE: 27 sts on larger size needles = 4 in (10 cm).

Adjust needle size to obtain correct gauge if necessary.

With smaller size circular, CO 80 (88, 94, 100, 100, 108, 116) sts. Join, being careful not to twist cast-on row; pm for beginning of rnd.

Work around in k1, p ribbing for 1¼ (1¼, 1¼, 1½, 2, 2, 2½) in [3 (3, 3, 4, 5, 5, 6) cm].

Change to larger size dpn. Knit 1 rnd, increasing 0 (0, 2, 4, 4, 4, 4) sts evenly spaced round = 80 (88, 96, 104, 104, 112, 120) sts.

Now continue in textured stripe pattern:

Knit 7 rnds, purl 1 rnd, knit 1 rnd, purl 1 rnd.

Rep these 10 rnds.

Continue in pattern until cap measures approx. 3¼ (3¾, 4, 4½, 5¼, 6, 6¾) in [8.5 (9.5, 10.5, 11.5, 13.5, 15.5, 17.5 cm] and then decrease on every 4th rnd. Decrease on odd-numbered rnds in pattern so you never decrease on a purl rnd.

Decrease Rnd 1: *K6, k2tog*; rep * to * around.

Decrease Rnd 2: *K5, k2tog*; rep * to * around.

Decrease Rnd 3: *K4, k2tog*; rep * to * around.

Decrease Rnd 4: *K2, k2tog*; rep * to * around, ending with k2 (3, 0, 1, 1, 2, 3).

Decrease Rnd 5: *K1, k2tog*; rep * to * around, ending with k2 (0, 0, 1, 1, 2, 0).

Decrease Rnd 6: *K2tog*; rep * to * around, ending with k0 (0, 0, 1, 1, 0, 0).

Continue in stockinette from now on.

Knit 1 rnd.

Next Rnd: K2tog*; rep * to * around, ending with k1 (0, 1, 1, 1, 0, 1).

Cut yarn and draw through rem sts; tighten.

FINISHING

Make a small pompom or buy a fake fur pompom. Attach securely to top of cap.

Weave in all ends neatly on WS.

Block by covering cap with a damp towel and leaving until completely dry.

Butterfly Cardigan

We knew that the butterfly, itself a symbol of summer, just had to be on one of our garments. This cardigan will vary in overall look depending on your color choices. We really like it paired with a summer dress!

SIZES: 1 (2, 4, 6, 8, 10 years)

FINISHED MEASUREMENTS:

Chest: Approx. 21¾ (22½, 24¾, 28, 29½, 30½) in [55 (57, 63, 71, 75, 77.5) cm]

Length: Approx.13 (15, 16½,18¼, 19½, 20½) in [33 (38, 42, 46.5, 49.5, 52) cm]

YARN: Sandnes Garn KlompeLompe Tynn merinoull (fine merino wool) [CYCA #1—fingering, 100% merino wool, 191 yd (175 m) / 50 g]

YARN COLORS AND AMOUNTS:

Color A (MC): Powder Rose 4032: 150 (150, 200, 200, 250, 300) g
Color B: Putty 1013: 50 (50, 50, 50, 50, 50, 50) g
Color C: Gray-Brown 2652: 50 (50, 50, 50, 50, 50, 50) g
Color D: Powder Pink 4344: 50 (50, 50, 50, 50, 50, 50) g

Needles: US sizes 1.5 and 2.5 (2.5 and 3 mm): 16 and 24 in (40 and 60 cm) circulars and sets of 5 dpn

NOTIONS: 7 (8, 8, 8, 9, 9) buttons

GAUGE: 27 sts on larger size needles = 4 in (10 cm).

Adjust needle size to obtain correct gauge if necessary.

The cardigan is worked from the top down, beginning back and forth.

With color A and smaller size circular, CO 91 (95, 101, 101, 109, 109) sts. Work back and forth in k1, p1 ribbing for 1¼ (¼, 1¼, 1⅜ , 1⅜, 1⅜) in [3 (3, 3, 3.5, 3.5, 3.5) cm].

Change to larger size circular and join to continue in the round. Knit 1 rnd, ending with CO 7 for steek.

NOTE: The steek sts are not included in stitch counts or shown on charts. Do not increase or decrease within the 7 steek sts.

Knit 1 rnd, increasing 46 (50, 44, 52, 52, 52) sts evenly spaced around = 137 (145, 145, 153, 161, 161) sts. Now begin following pattern chart for chosen size. After completing charted rows, you should have 239 (253, 253, 305, 321, 321) sts, Knit 0 (4, 3, 5, 8, 8) rnds with MC. Knit 1 rnd, increasing 8 (6, 26, 0, 0, 12) sts evenly spaced around = 247 (259, 279, 305, 321, 333) sts. For size 4 years, knit 4 rnds. For sizes 8 (10) years, knit 4 (6) rnds.

Set aside sleeve sts as follows:
K33 (34, 38, 43, 46, 47), place next 56 (60, 62, 64, 66, 69) sts on a holder, CO 7 sts for underarm, k69 (71, 79, 91, 97, 101), place next 56 (60, 62, 64, 66, 69) sts on a holder, CO 7 sts for underarm, k33 (34, 38, 43, 46, 47).

Sizes 6 (8, 10) years

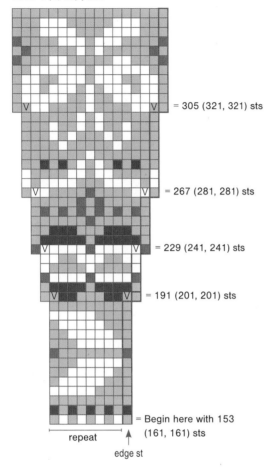

= 305 (321, 321) sts

= 267 (281, 281) sts

= 229 (241, 241) sts

= 191 (201, 201) sts

= Begin here with 153 (161, 161) sts

repeat

↑ edge st

Sizes 1 (2, 4) years

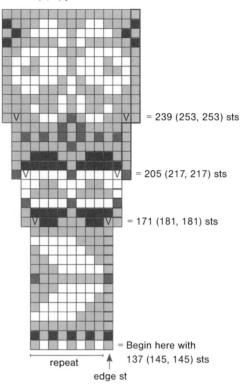

= 239 (253, 253) sts

= 205 (217, 217) sts

= 171 (181, 181) sts

= Begin here with 137 (145, 145) sts

repeat

↑ edge st

Color A

Color B

Color C

Color D

V Increase here with M1 (lift strand between 2 sts and knit into back loop with color shown in square)

FRONT AND BACK

You should now have 149 (153, 169, 191, 203, 209) sts on needle. Work in stockinette with MC until body measures 11¾ (13¾, 15½, 17, 18¼, 19) in [30 (35, 39, 43, 46, 48) cm]. Knit 1 rnd and, *at the same time*, BO steek sts. Change to smaller size circular. Work back and forth in k1, p1 ribbing for 1¼ 1¼, 1¼, 1⅜, 1⅜, 1½) in [3 (3, 3, 3.5, 3.5, 4) cm]. BO in ribbing on last row.

SLEEVES

With color A and smaller size dpn, CO 4 sts, knit the held 56 (60, 62, 64, 66, 69) sleeve sts, CO 3 sts. Divide sts onto dpn and join to work in the round. Mark 1st st for center of sleeve; always purl marked st.

When sleeve measures ¾ in (2 cm), begin shaping sleeve: P1 (marked st), k2tog, knit until 2 sts rem before marked st, sl 1, k1, psso.

Rep this decrease rnd every ¾ (¾, ¾, 1, 1, 1¼) in [2 (2, 2, 2.5, 2.5, 3) cm until 45 (49, 49, 51, 51, 56) sts rem. Continue without decreasing until sleeve is 7½ (8¾, 9¾, 10¾, 12¼, 13½) in [19 (22, 25, 27, 31, 34) cm] long. Knit 1 rnd, decreasing 1 (1, 1, 1, 1, 0) sts.

Change to smaller size dpn and work around in k1, p1 ribbing for 1¼ 1¼, 1¼, 1⅜, 1⅜, 1½) in [3 (3, 3, 3.5, 3.5, 4) cm]. BO in ribbing.

FINISHING

Reinforce steek by machine-stitching two fine lines on each side of center steek st. Carefully cut steek open up center st. Work buttonholes on right side for girl's version and on left for boy's.

Button band: With smaller size circular and color A, pick up and knit approx. 3 sts for every 4 rows up front edge. Work 8 rows in k1, p1 ribbing. BO in ribbing, making sure bind-off is not too tight.

Buttonhole band: Work as for button band, but, on 3rd row, make 7 (8, 8, 8, 9, 9) buttonholes evenly spaced on band. For each buttonhole, BO 2 sts and CO 2 new sts over gap on 4th row.

Fold in cut edges and sew down on WS with small stitches. If it is difficult to make a fine edge, you can knit a facing to sew over each cut edge. Pick up and knit sts as for front band. Work back and forth in stockinette until facing covers cut edge. BO and, with MC, sew down facing on WS. Using MC to sew down facing keeps facing invisible.

Weave in all ends neatly on WS.
Sew on buttons.
Block by covering sweater with a damp towel and leaving until completely dry.

Butterfly Cap

Those of us living on the island of Karmøy are accustomed to always having a cap handy, even during the summer holidays. This cap is knitted with fine yarn and has a pattern that perfectly matches the Butterfly Cardigan.

SIZES: 6-12 months (1-2, 3-6, 8-12 years)

YARN: Sandnes Garn KlompeLompe Tynn merinoull (fine merino wool) [CYCA #1—fingering, 100% merino wool, 191 yd (175 m) / 50 g]

YARN COLORS AND AMOUNTS:
Color A: Soft Purple 4331: 50 (50, 50, 50) g
Color B: Putty1013: 50 (50, 50, 50) g or small amounts

NEEDLES: US sizes 1.5 and 2.5 (2.5 and 3 mm): 16 in (40 cm) circulars and sets of 5 dpn

GAUGE: 27 sts on larger size needles = 4 in (10 cm).

Adjust needle size to obtain correct gauge if necessary.

With color A and smaller size circular or dpn, CO 92 (100, 108, 116) sts. Join, being careful not to twist cast-on row; pm for beginning of rnd. Work around in k1, p1 ribbing for 1¼ (1¼, 1¼, 1¼) in [3 (3, 3, 3) cm].

Change to larger size circular. Knit 1 rnd, increasing 20 sts evenly spaced around = 112 (120, 128, 136) sts.

Pm as follows: k30 (34, 48, 42), pm, k17, pm, knit to end of rnd.

NOW SET UP PATTERN:

Rnd 1: *K1 with color A, k1 with color B*; rep * to * around except for the 17 sts between markers – knit these 17 sts following chart.

Rnd 2: *K1 with color B, k1 with color A*; rep * to * around except for the 17 sts between markers – knit these 17 sts following chart.

Rep Rnds 1-2 until charted rows have been completed.

Continue in stockinette with color A only until cap measures approx. 5¼ (6, 7, 8) in [13 (15, 18, 20) cm].

Shape crown as follows:

NOTE: Change to dpn when sts no longer fit around circular.

Decrease Rnd 1: *K6, k2tog*; rep * to * around = 98 (105, 112, 119) sts rem.
Knit 3 rnds.

Decrease Rnd 2: *K5, k2tog*; rep * to * around = 84 (90, 96, 102) sts rem.
Knit 2 rnds.

Decrease Rnd 3: *K4, k2tog*; rep * to * around = 70 (75, 80, 85) sts rem.
Knit 2 rnds.

Decrease Rnd 4: *K3, k2tog*; rep * to * around = 56 (60, 64, 68) sts rem.
Knit 2 rnds.

Decrease Rnd 5: *K6, k2tog*; rep * to * around, ending with k0 (4, 0, 4) = 49 (53, 56, 60) sts rem.
Knit 2 rnds.

Decrease Rnd 6: *K5, k2tog*; rep * to * around, ending with k0 (4, 0, 4) = 42 (46, 48, 52) sts rem.
Knit 1 rnd.

Decrease Rnd 7: *K4, k2tog*; rep * to * around, ending with k0 (4, 0, 4) = 35 (39, 40, 44) sts rem.
Knit 1 rnd.

Decrease Rnd 8: *K3, k2tog*; rep * to * around, ending with k0 (4, 0, 4) = 28 (32, 32, 36) sts rem.
Knit 1 rnd.

Decrease Rnd 9: *K2, k2tog*; rep * to * around = 21 (24, 24, 27) sts rem.
Knit 1 rnd.

Last Decrease Rnd: K2tog around, ending with k1 (0, 0, 1).

Cut yarn and draw end through rem sts; tighten.

FINISHING
Weave in all ends neatly on WS.
Block by covering cap with a damp towel and leaving until completely dry.

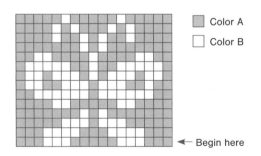

Color A
Color B

← Begin here

Butterfly Cardigan: color A: 6521, color B: 1013, color C: 7251, color D: 6571

Tulla Skirt and Tulla Doll Skirt: color 6571

David Doll Sweater-Jacket: color 6521

Wing Sweater-Jacket:
KlompeLompe Tynn merinoull,
color A: 4344

Butterfly Headband

Make a headband with the same pattern as the Butterfly Cardigan.

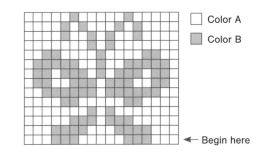

Color A
Color B

← Begin here

SIZES: 6-12 months (1-2, 3-6, 8-12 years)
YARN: Sandnes Garn KlompeLompe Tynn merinoull (fine merino wool) [CYCA #1—fingering, 100% merino wool, 191 yd (175 m) / 50 g]
YARN COLORS AND AMOUNTS:
Color A: Putty 1013: 50 (50, 50, 50) g
Color B: Soft Purple 4331: 50 (50, 50, 50) g
NEEDLES: US sizes 1.5 and 2.5 (2.5 and 3 mm): 16 in (40 cm) circulars
GAUGE: 27 sts on larger size needles = 4 in (10 cm).
Adjust needle size to obtain correct gauge if necessary.

With color A and smaller size circular, CO 92 (100, 108, 116) sts. Join, being careful not to twist cast-on row; pm for beginning of rnd. Work around in k1, p1 ribbing for ¾ (¾, ¾, ¾) in [2 (2, 2, 2) cm].

Change to larger size circular. Knit 1 rnd, increasing 20 sts evenly spaced around = 112 (120, 128, 136) sts.

Pm as follows: k30 (34, 48, 42), pm, k17, pm, knit to end of rnd.

Now work 0 (3, 3, 5) rnds, repeating Rnds 1-2:
Rnd 1: *K1 with color A, k1 with color B*; rep * to * around.

Rnd 2: *K1 with color B, k1 with color A*; rep * to * around.

Continue:
Rnd 1: *K1 with color A, k1 with color B*; rep * to * around except for the 17 sts between markers – knit these 17 sts following chart.
Rnd 2: *K1 with color B, k1 with color A*; rep * to * around except for the 17 sts between markers – knit these17 sts following chart.
Rep Rnds 1-2 until charted rows have been completed.

Now work 0 (3, 3, 5) rnds, repeating Rnds 1-2:
Rnd 1: *K1 with color A, k1 with color B*; rep * to * around.
Rnd 2: *K1 with color B, k1 with color A*; rep * to * around.

Knit 1 rnd with color A, decreasing 20 sts evenly spaced around = 92 (100, 108, 116) sts rem.
Change to smaller size circular and work around in k1, p1 ribbing for ¾ (¾, ¾, ¾) in [2 (2, 2, 2) cm].
BO loosely in ribbing on last rnd.

FINISHING
Weave in all ends neatly on WS.
Block by covering headband with a damp towel and leaving until completely dry.

Eivind Sweater-Jacket

If you can choose only one project to knit, this sweater-jacket would be ideal. The Eivind jacket works just as well over a dressy outfit as it does for daycare or school.

SIZES: 6 months (1, 2, 4, 6, 8, 10 years)
FINISHED MEASUREMENTS:
Chest: Approx. 21½ (23, 23, 24½, 26, 28¾, 29½) in [54.5 (58.5, 58.5, 62, 66, 73, 75) cm]
Total length: Approx. 12¾ (13, 14¼, 15½, 17¼, 18½, 20½) in [32 (33, 36, 39, 44, 47, 52) cm]
YARN: Sandnes Garn KlompeLompe merinoull [CYCA #3 – DK, light worsted, 100% merino wool, 114 yd (104 m) / 50 g]
YARN COLORS AND AMOUNTS:
Gray-Blue 6061: 200 (200, 250, 300, 300, 350, 400) g
NEEDLES: US sizes 2.5 and 4 (3 and 3.5 mm): 16 and 24 in (40 and 60 cm) circulars (or magic loop), sets of 5 dpn
NOTIONS: 7 (7, 8, 8, 9, 9, 10) buttons
GAUGE: 22 sts on larger size needles = 4 in (10 cm).
Adjust needle size to obtain correct gauge if necessary.

The sweater is worked from the top down, back and forth on a circular needle.

With smaller size circular, CO 65 (69, 69, 73, 75, 77, 79) sts. Work back and forth in k1, p1 ribbing for 6 (6, 6, 8, 8, 10, 10, 10) rows.

Change to larger size circular. Work the sleeves and the two front pieces in seed st and the back in stockinette.

Seed Stitch
Row 1: *K1, p1*; rep * to * across.
All Subsequent Rows: Work purl over knit and knit over purl.

Divide body for raglan shaping:
10 (11, 11, 11, 11, 12, 13) seed sts, yo, k1 (marked st for raglan), yo, 9 (9, 9, 9, 10, 10, 10) seed sts, yo, k1 (marked st for raglan), yo, k23 (25, 25, 29, 29, 29, 29), yo, k1 (marked st for raglan), yo, 9 (9, 9, 9, 10, 10, 10) seed sts, yo, k1 (marked st for raglan), yo, 10 (11, 11, 11, 11, 12, 13) seed sts.

Next Row (WS): Work as est but, work each yarnover through back loop in pattern as knit or purl.

Continue to work a yarnover on each side of the four marked sts on every RS row. On WS rows, work each yarnover through back loop in pattern as knit or purl. Work marked sts as knit on RS and purl on WS.

After increasing 15 (16, 16, 17, 19, 21, 23) times, you should have 185 (197, 197, 209, 227, 245, 263) sts total.

Next Row: Continue in seed st on sleeves and fronts, but, do not increase. Instead, bind off each marked st.

David Rompers and Newborn Cap:
KlompeLompe Tynn merinoull, color 2652

Place the front and back sts on same needle and CO 6 sts at each underarm = 115 (123, 123, 131, 139, 149, 159) sts.

Place rem 39 (41, 41, 43, 48, 52, 56) sts for each sleeve on separate holders.

Pm at center of the 6 sts of each underarm. Continue in seed st on fronts and stockinette on back.
Work as est until body measures 11½ (11¾, 12¾, 13¾, 15½, 16½, 18½) in [29 (30, 32, 35, 39, 42, 47) cm] down center back.
Change to smaller size needle and work in k1, p1 ribbing for 1¼ (1¼, 1½, 1½, 2, 2, 2) in [3 (3, 4, 4, 5, 5, 5) cm].

Sleeves
With larger size dpn, CO 3 sts, work the held 39 (41, 41, 43, 48, 52, 56) sts, CO 3 sts. You are now at center of underarm. Divide sts onto dpn and join.

Work around in seed st. After ¾ in (2 cm), begin shaping sleeve: 1 seed st, k2tog, continue as est until 3 sts rem, sl 1, k1 psso, 1 seed st. Decrease the same way every ¾ (¾, 1, 1⅜, 1, 1, ¾) in [2 (2, 2.5, 3.5, 2.5, 2.5, 2) cm] until 31 (31, 31, 35, 34, 36, 36) sts rem.
Sizes 6 months (1, 2, 4 years) only: Decrease 1 st on last rnd.

When sleeve is 6¼ (7½, 8¾, 9¾, 10¾, 12¼, 13½) in [16 (19, 22, 25, 27, 31, 34) cm] long, change to smaller size dpn and work around in k1, p1 ribbing for 1¼ (1¼, 1½, 1½, 2, 2, 2) in [3 (3, 4, 4, 5, 5, 5) cm]; BO on ribbing on last rnd.

Button/Buttonhole Bands
Left Front: With smaller size needle, pick up and knit 3 sts for every 4 rows along front edge. Work back and forth in k1, p1 ribbing. On Row 4, make 7 (7, 8, 8, 9, 9, 10) buttonholes evenly spaced on band. For each buttonhole, k2tog, yo. Work 3 more rows ribbing, binding off on last row.

Right Front: Work as for left front, omitting buttonholes.

FINISHING
Seam underarms. Sew on buttons. Weave in all ends neatly on WS.
Block by covering sweater with a damp towel and leaving it until completely dry or gently steam press sweater under a damp pressing cloth.

Wing Sweater-Jacket: KlompeLompe, Tynn merinoull, color 1013

Lace Tights: KlompeLompe, Tynn merinoull, color 4331

Billie Cap

A cap knitted in a new way—sideways, back and forth on a circular needle.

SIZES: 0-1 (1-3, 3-6, 9-12 months, 2-3, 4-7, 8-10 years)

YARN: Sandnes Garn KlompeLompe Tynn merinoull (fine merino wool) [CYCA #1—fingering, 100% merino wool, 191 yd (175 m) / 50 g]

YARN COLORS AND AMOUNTS:
Color 4331: 50 (50, 50, 50, 50, 100, 100) g

NEEDLES: US sizes 1.5 and 2.5 (2.5 and 3 mm): 16 in (40 cm) circulars and sets of 5 dpn or 32 in (80 cm) magic loop circular

GAUGE: 27 sts on larger size needles = 4 in (10 cm).

Adjust needle size to obtain correct gauge if necessary.

The cap begins at the side in garter stitch ridges and is worked back and forth.

With larger size circular, CO 26 (30, 36, 40, 44, 48, 52) sts.
NOTE: When turning, slip first st after the turn and tighten yarn a bit.

SIZES 0-1 (1-3, 3-6, 9-12) MONTHS:
*Knit 4 rows.
Knit until 2 sts rem; turn, knit to end of row.
Knit until 4 sts rem; turn, knit to end of row.
Knit until 6 sts rem; turn, knit to end of row.

Knit until 8 sts rem; turn, knit to end of row.
Knit until 10 sts rem; turn, knit to end of row.*
Rep * to * 12 (13, 14, 14) times.

SIZES 2-3 (4-7, 8-10) YEARS:
*Knit 4 rows.
Knit until 2 sts rem; turn, knit to end of row.
Knit until 4 sts rem; turn, knit to end of row.
Knit until 6 sts rem; turn, knit to end of row.
Knit until 8 sts rem; turn, knit to end of row.
Knit until 10 sts rem; turn, knit to end of row.
Knit until 12 sts rem; turn, knit to end of row.*

Rep * to * 14 (15, 16) times.

ALL SIZES:
Last Row: BO knitwise. Cut yarn, leaving long enough end to seam cap.

FINISHING
Seam cap.

With larger size dpn or magic loop needle, pick up and knit 24 (26, 28, 28, 28, 30, 30) sts around top of cap. Join and pm for beginning of rnd.
Purl 1 rnd.
Decrease Rnd 1: *P2tog*; rep * to * around.

Color Blue 7251 and Pink 4331

Decrease Rnd 2: *P2tog*; rep * to * around, ending with
p0 (1, 0, 0, 0, 1, 1).
Cut yarn and draw end through rem sts; tighten.

With smaller size dpn or magic loop needle, pick up and
knit 84 (90, 94, 98, 108, 112, 120) sts around bottom of
cap. Join and pm for beginning of rnd.
Work in k1, p1 ribbing for 10 (10, 10, 10, 12, 12, 14) rnds.
BO in ribbing on last rnd, making sure bind-off is neither
too tight nor too loose.

Weave in all ends neatly on WS.
Block by covering cap with a damp towel and leaving until
completely dry

Butterfly Cap: color A 1013, color B: 4032
David Sweater-Jacket: 4032
Billie Shorts: color 2652

Billie Shorts ⟶ ⟫

Billie Shorts

Delightful garter-stitch shorts, knitted sideways.
Use an I-cord or a leather cord at the waist.

SIZES: 0-1 (3, 6, 12, 18-24 months)

YARN: Sandnes Garn KlompeLompe Tynn merinoull (fine merino wool) [CYCA #1—fingering, 100% merino wool, 191 yd (175 m) / 50 g]

YARN COLORS AND AMOUNTS:
Blue-Petroleum 7251: 50 (50, 100, 100, 100) g

NEEDLES: US sizes 1.5 and 2.5 (2.5 and 3 mm): 16 in (40 cm) circulars and sets of 5 dpn or 32 in (80 cm) magic loop circular

GAUGE: 27 sts on larger size needles = 4 in (10 cm).

Adjust needle size to obtain correct gauge if necessary.

The shorts, worked back and forth, begin at the side with garter stitch ridges.

With larger size circular, CO 20 (24, 28, 32, 38) sts. Knit back and forth for 2¾ (3¼, 3½, 4, 4¼) in [7 (8, 9, 10, 11) cm].

Next Row (RS): Knit until 1 st rem, M1, k1.
Knit 1 row on WS. Rep these 2 rows 8 times total.

Next Row: Knit and CO 5 sts at end of row.
Work in garter st without increasing for 1½ in (4 cm).

Next Row (WS): BO the first 5 sts.

Next, Decrease, Row: Knit until 3 sts rem, k2tog, k1.
Knit 1 row on WS.
Rep these 2 rows 8 times total.

Knit back and forth for 2¾ (3¼, 3½, 4, 4¼) in [7 (8, 9, 10, 11) cm] without decreasing.

Now raise back with increases, beginning on RS.
K1, M1, knit to end of row.
Knit 3 rows.
Rep these 4 rows 2 times total.

Work in garter st for 0 (⅜, ¾, 1¼, 1½) in [0 (1, 2, 3, 4) cm].

Next Row (RS): Knit until 1 st rem, M1, k1.
Knit 1 row on WS.
Rep these 2 rows 20 times total.

Work in garter st for 1½ in (4 cm) without increasing.

Next, Decrease, Row: Knit until 3 sts rem, k2tog, k1.

Knit 1 row on WS.
Rep these 2 rows 20 times total.

Work in garter st for 0 (³/₈, ³/₄, 1¼, 1½) in [0 (1, 2, 3, 4) cm].

Knit 2 rows.

Next, Decrease, Row (RS): K1, k2tog, knit to end of row.
Knit 3 rows.
Next, Decrease, Row (WS): K1, k2tog, knit to end of row.
Last Row: BO knitwise.

Seam side and crotch.

LEG BANDS
With smaller size dpn, beginning at crotch, pick up and knit 3 sts for every 4 rows around leg.
Knit 1 rnd, adjusting stitch count to 60 (70, 80, 80, 84) sts.
Purl 1 row.
Next Row: K20 (25, 30, 30, 32), *k2tog*; rep * to * 10 times, k20 (25, 30, 30, 32).
Purl 1 row.
Loosely BO knitwise.

WAIST BAND
With smaller size circular, beginning at center back, pick up and knit approx. 1 st in every other st. Knit 1 rnd, adjusting stitch count to 100 (110, 120, 130, 140) sts. Work 6 rnds in k1, p1 ribbing.
Next Rnd, Eyelets: Work 4 (4, 5, 5, 6) sts in ribbing, k2tog, yo, *rib 8 (9, 10, 11, 12), k2tog, yo,*; rep * to * a total of 9 times, work 4 (5, 5, 6, 6) sts in ribbing
Work 6 rnds in k1, p1 ribbing. BO in ribbing on last rnd.

FINISHING
Weave in all ends neatly on WS.
Thread cord through waistband eyelets.
Block by covering shorts with a damp towel and leaving until completely dry.

Pocket Dress ———————— »

Pocket Dress

A simple dress with fun pocket details.

SIZES: 6 months (1, 2, 4, 6, 8, 10 years)

FINISHED MEASUREMENTS:
Chest: Approx. 16¼ (18¼, 19¾, 21, 22½, 24, 24) in [41 (46, 50, 53.5, 57, 61, 61) cm]
Total length: Approx. 16¼ (18¼, 20½, 22¾, 25¼, 27½, 29½) in [41 (46, 52, 58, 64, 70, 75) cm]

YARN: Sandnes Garn Duo (fine merino wool) [CYCA #3 – DK, light worsted, 55% merino wool, 45% cotton, 126 yd (115 m) / 50 g]

YARN COLORS AND AMOUNTS:
MC: Color Gray-Brown 2652: 150 (200, 200, 200, 250, 250, 300) g
CC: Color Powder Rose 4032: 50 (50, 50, 50, 50, 50, 50) g
OR reverse MC and CC colors: 4032 (MC) + 2652 (CC)

NEEDLES: US sizes 2.5 and 4 (3 and 3.5 mm): 16 in (40 cm) or [24 in (60 cm) in larger size] circulars and sets of 5 dpn; optional 32 in (80) cm circular for magic loop

NOTIONS: 3 (3, 3, 4, 4, 4, 4) buttons

GAUGE: 22 sts on larger size needles = 4 in (10 cm).

Adjust needle size to obtain correct gauge if necessary.

The dress begins with a doubled bib at the back and is worked back and forth on a circular.

BIB
With smaller size circular and MC, CO 36 (40, 42, 44, 46, 48, 48) sts. Work back and forth in stockinette for 2½ (2¾, 3¼, 3½, 3½, 4, 4¼) in [6 (7, 8, 9, 9, 10, 11) cm]. Place sts on a holder or spare needle. Fold and seam sides.

DOUBLE STRAPS
Right Strap:
With RS facing and with dpn, pick up and knit 6 sts along top of bib (beginning at fold) and CO 6 sts = 12 sts. Divide sts onto dpn (or use magic loop) and join.

NOTE:
We recommend you use magic loop if you know the technique. That way, you can pick up and knit 6 sts on the back instead of casting on 6 sts on the needles. See a video for magic loop at klompelompe.no

Knit 7 (7, 8, 8, 9, 10, 10) rnds in stockinette.
Next, Increase, Rnd: K1, M1 (lift strand between 2 sts and knit into back loop), knit until 1 st rem, M1, k1.
Continue in stockinette, increasing on every 4th rnd until there are 28 (32, 34, 36, 38, 40, 40) sts.
Work around in stockinette without increasing for 2½ (2¾, 3¼, 3½, 3½, 4, 4¼) in [6 (7, 8, 9, 9, 10, 11) cm].

Place the first 14 (16, 17, 18, 19, 20, 20) sts on one needle and the next 14 (16, 17, 18, 19, 20, 20) sts on another needle. Use a <page 58> third needle to join the two sets of sts (*k2tog with first st of each needle*; rep * to * to end of row) = 14 (16, 17, 18, 19, 20, 20) sts rem. Leave sts on needle.

Left Strap:
With RS facing and with dpn, CO 6 sts, pick up and knit 6 sts at left side of bib = 12 sts. Work as for right strap but, when you've worked 2½ (2¾, 3¼, 3½, 3½, 4, 4¼) in [6 (7, 8, 9, 9, 10, 11) cm] in stockinette, k14 (16, 17, 18, 19, 20, 20) before you knit the sts on front and back together.

Join the pieces as follows:
Beginning on RS, with smaller size needle, knit right strap, CO 13 (15, 17, 19, 21, 23, 23) sts, knit sts from bib, CO 13 (15, 17, 19, 21, 23, 23) sts, knit sts of left strap. Join to work in the round = 90 (102, 110, 118, 126, 134, 134) sts.

Work 3 rnds with stockinette all around except for the 13 (15, 17, 19, 21, 23, 23) sts on each underarm which are worked in k1, p1 ribbing.

Change to larger size needle and stockinette only. Knit 1 rnd, increasing 28 sts evenly spaced around = 118 (130, 138, 146, 154, 162, 162) sts. Knit 8 rnds. Knit 1 rnd, increasing 28 sts evenly spaced around = 146 (158, 166, 174, 182, 190, 190) sts.

From this point on, take all measurements from the shoulder down.

When dress measures 7½ (8¼, 9¾, 11, 12¼, 13½, 14½) in [19 (21, 25, 28, 31, 34, 37) cm], make openings for the pockets. K45 (48, 50, 52, 54, 56, 56); turn. P90 (96, 100, 104, 108, 112, 112); turn.
Work back and forth on the 90 (96, 100, 104, 108, 112, 112) sts for back and place rem 56 (62, 66, 70, 74, 78, 78) sts for front on a holder.

Work back sts for approx. 3¼ (3¼, 3½, 3½, 4, 4, 4) in [8 (8, 9, 9, 10, 10, 10) cm], ending with a WS row. K45 (48, 50, 52, 54, 56, 56) (you are now at center back). Leave sts on holder.

Work the same way as for back on the held 56 (62, 66, 70, 74, 78, 78) sts, but, begin by working on all the sts and end with a WS row.

Continue around on all sts until piece measures 16¼ (18¼, 20½, 22¾, 25¼, 27½, 29½) in [41 (46, 52, 58, 64, 70, 75) cm].
Knit 1 rnd, decreasing 28 sts evenly spaced around.
Knit 1 rnd.
Change to CC.
Knit 1 rnd.
Purl 1 rnd.
Knit 3 rnds, binding off on last rnd.

POCKETS

With CC, begin at left side of pocket opening. With smaller size needle, pick up and knit 20 (20, 24, 24, 26, 26, 26) sts on each side = 40 (20, 48, 48, 52, 52, 52) sts.
Pm on each side with 20 (20, 24, 24, 26, 26, 26) sts between each marker. Join to work in the round.
Knit 3 rnds.
Decrease/Increase Rnd: K1, sl 1, k1, psso, knit until 2 st before marker, M1, k2, M1, knit until 3 sts rem, k2tog, k1.

Continue around in stockinette, repeating Decrease/Increase Rnd every 3rd rnd a total of 5 (6, 7, 8, 9, 10, 10) times.

Knit 2 rnds.

Decrease Rnd: *Sl 1, k1, psso, sl 1, k1, psso, knit until 4 sts before marker, k2tog, k2tog*; rep * to * around.

Rep the Decrease Rnd.

On next rnd, bind off knitwise. Seam lower part of each pocket and tack pocket to dress with MC at a couple of points.

FINISHING
Sew on back of bib; fold lower edge and sew down with MC. Weave in all ends neatly on WS.

Make ties for back:
Thread a strand of yarn into one side of back opening. Twist the strand into a cord while it is attached to the dress. Knot one end. Make another cord the same way on other side. On the three largest sizes, you might want to make one more cord to attach in middle of back opening.

Block by covering dress with a damp towel and leaving it until completely dry or gently steam-press dress under a damp pressing cloth.

Spinnvill Hooded Jacket

A nice and soft hooded jacket knitted with merino wool yarn. Special features include a zipper sewn up the front and a large, roomy hood.

SIZES: 1 (2, 4, 6, 8, 10) years

FINISHED MEASUREMENTS:

Chest: Approx. 22¾ (23¾, 25½, 28, 30, 32¼) in [58 (60, 65, 71, 76, 82) cm]

Total length: Approx. 12¼ (14¼, 16¼, 18¼, 20, 22) in [31 (36, 41, 46, 51, 56) cm]

YARN: Sandnes Garn KlompeLompe merinoull [CYCA #3 – DK, light worsted, 100% merino wool, 114 yd (104 m) / 50 g]

YARN COLORS AND AMOUNTS:

Blue Petroleum 7251: 300 (300, 350, 400, 450, 550) g

NEEDLES: US sizes 2.5 and 4 (3 and 3.5 mm): 24 in (60 cm) circulars, sets of 5 dpn

NOTIONS: Separating zipper 11¾ (13¾, 15¾, 17¾, 19¾, 21¾) in [30, 35, 40, 45, 50, 55) cm] long

GAUGE: 22 sts on larger size needles = 4 in (10 cm).

Adjust needle size to obtain correct gauge if necessary.

The sweater is worked from the top down, back and forth on a circular needle.

With smaller size circular, CO 128 (132, 144, 156, 168 180) sts. Work back and forth in k1, p1 ribbing for 10 (10, 12, 12, 14, 14) rows.

Change to larger size circular. CO 7 sts for steek.
NOTE: The steek sts are not included in stitch counts or shown on charts. Do not increase or decrease within the 7 steek sts.

Now work around in stockinette until body measures 8¼ (9¾, 11½, 13½, 13½, 15) in [21 (25, 29, 34, 34, 38) cm]. K28 (29, 32, 35, 38, 41), BO 8 sts, k56 (58, 64, 70, 76, 82), BO 8 sts, k28 (29, 32, 35, 38, 41).

SLEEVES (MAKE TWO ALIKE)

With smaller size dpn, CO 34 (34, 34, 38, 40 40) sts. Divide sts onto dpn and join. Work 12 rnds (all sizes) in k1, p1 ribbing. Change to larger size dpn and work around in stockinette. After 1 rnd, increase as follows: K1, M1, knit until 1 st rem, M1, k1. Increase the same way every 1¼ in (3 cm) until there are 46 (48, 50, 54, 58, 62) sts. Continue in stockinette until sleeve is 8 (9½, 10¾, 11¾, 12¾, 13½) in [20 (24, 27, 30, 32, 34) cm] long. BO 8 sts centered on underarm = 38 (40, 42, 46, 50, 54) sts rem.

YOKE

Arrange pieces on larger size circular: knit sts of right front, one sleeve, back, second sleeve, left front. Pm at each intersection of body and sleeve = 188 (196, 212, 232, 252, 272) sts total.

RAGLAN SHAPING

Raglan Decrease Rnd: Knit until 3 stitches before marker. *K1, sl 1, k1, psso, knit until 3 sts before next marker, k2tog, k1*; rep * to * around = 8 sts decreased around. Decrease the same way on every other rnd.

After 13 (14, 15 , 17, 19, 21) decrease rnds = 84 (84, 92, 96, 100, 104) sts rem. BO the 7 steek sts and begin hood, working back and forth.

HOOD

Continue without decreasing. The next rnd is the RS. Increase 10 sts evenly spaced across back (between the two raglan markers for back). Work the hood in stockinette with garter st on the 4 outermost sts at each side until hood measures 10¾ (11, 11½, 11¾, 11¾, 12¾) in [27 (28, 29, 30, 30, 32) cm] from last raglan decrease rnd. You can either bind off at this point or join top of hood with Kitchener st. Seam shoulders.

Weave in all ends neatly on WS.
Machine-stitch two fine lines on each side of center steek st. Carefully cut up center steek st. Chain stitch on each side of zipper or stitch as shown in picture. Sew these stitches securely into jacket to attach zipper.
If cut edges do not look good, make a facing: pick up and knit sts along cut edge and work in stockinette until facing covers raw edges. Sew down facing on WS.

FINISHING

Seam underarms.
Block by covering sweater with a damp towel and leaving it until completely dry.

Blueberry Girl's Summer Kerchief

A kerchief knitted with fine yarn. Perfect for keeping ears warm while the breeze caresses baby's neck as she relaxes outside. The kerchief also enhances a dressy outfit or party dress

SIZES: 3-6 (6-12 months, 1-2, 3-5 years)

YARN: Sandnes Garn KlompeLompe Tynn merinoull (fine merino wool) [CYCA #1—fingering, 100% merino wool, 191 yd (175 m) / 50 g]

YARN COLORS AND AMOUNTS:
Blue-Petroleum 7251: 50 (50, 50, 50) g

NEEDLES: US sizes 1.5 and 2.5 (2.5 and 3 mm): 16 or 24 in (40 or 60 cm) circulars; 2 dpn in smaller size for I-cord

GAUGE: 27 sts on larger size needles = 4 in (10 cm).

Adjust needle size to obtain correct gauge if necessary.

With smaller size circular, CO 85 (89, 93, 97) sts. Work 10 rows in stockinette (= knit on RS and purl on WS); the 1st row = RS.
Next Row (picot foldline): *K2tog, yo*; rep * to * across, ending with k1.
Work 11 rows in stockinette.

Change to large size needle.
Work 8 rows in stockinette.
Lace Row 1: K1 (3, 5, 2), k2tog, yo, *k8, k2tog, yo*; rep * to * across until 2 (4, 6, 3) sts rem, k2 (4, 6, 3).

Work 9 rows in stockinette.
Lace Row 2: K6 (8, 10, 7), k2tog, yo, *k8, k2tog, yo*; rep * to * across until 7 (9, 11, 8) sts rem, k7 (9, 11, 8).
Work 5 (9, 11, 13) rows in stockinette and lace—with a lace row on every 10th row, staggering lace holes as above.

Now continue in stockinette and lace, but add side bands (work the outermost 5 sts at each side in seed st: k1, p1 on first row and work purl over knit and knit over purl on subsequent rows) and decrease: Work 5 seed sts, k2tog, stockinette (with lace as est) until 7 sts rem, sl 1, k1, psso, 5 seed sts. Rep the decreases on every RS row.

When 3 sts rem between the seed st bands and you are on a RS row, work Kerchief Tip Rows:

Row 1: 5 seed sts, sl 1, k2tog, psso, 5 seed sts.

Row 2: 5 seed sts, p1, 5 seed sts.

Row 3: 4 seed sts, sl 1, k2tog, psso, 4 seed sts.

Row 4: 9 seed sts.

Row 5: 3 seed sts, sl 1 purlwise, p2tog, psso, 3 seed sts.

Wing Cardigan: KlompeLompe Tynn merinoull, color 606

Row 6: 7 seed sts.

Row 7: 2 seed sts, sl 1, k2tog, psso, 2 seed sts.

Row 8: 5 seed sts.

Row 9: 1 seed st, sl 1 purlwise, p2tog, psso, 1 seed st.

Row 10: Sl 1 purlwise, p2tog, psso.
Cut yarn, draw end through rem sts and tighten.
Weave in all ends neatly on WS. Before adding ribbing around neck, gently steam-press kerchief under a damp pressing cloth.

With smaller size needle, pick up and knit 29 (33, 35, 37) sts along one side of neck, CO 15 (15, 15, 17) sts, pick up and knit 29 (33, 35, 37) sts along other side of neck = 73 (81, 85, 91) sts total.

Work 8 rows in k1, p1 ribbing. On last row, BO in ribbing except for the first 4 and last 4 sts. These sts will be used for I-cord ties. On each side of ribbing, use rem 4 sts to knit an I-cord (see below) about 7 in (18 cm) long.

I-CORD: Using dpn, knit across, *slide sts back to front of needle without turning. Knit across, pulling yarn across WS.* Rep * to * until cord is desired length. Cut yarn, draw end through rem sts and tighten.

Gurine Vest ——————— ≫

Gurine Vest

A fun vest with exciting details on the back.
Nice and cozy on those cooler summer days.

SIZES: 3-6 (6-9 months, 1, 2, 4, 6, 8, 10 years)

FINISHED MEASUREMENTS:
Chest: Approx. 16½ (18, 19¼, 21½, 22¾, 24½, 25¾, 27¼)
in [42 (45.5, 49, 54.5, 58, 62, 65.5, 69) cm]
Total length: Approx. 9 (10¾, 11½, 13½, 15½, 16½, 19¼,
20½) in [23 (27, 29, 34, 39, 42, 49, 52) cm]

YARN: Sandnes Garn KlompeLompe Spøt [CYCA #3 – DK,
light worsted, 40% merino wool, 40% alpaca, 20% nylon, 147
yd (134 m) / 50 g]

YARN COLORS AND AMOUNTS:
Color 4321: 50 (100, 100 100, 100, 150, 150, 150) g

NEEDLES: US sizes 2.5 and 4 (3 and 3.5 mm): 16 and 24 in
(40 and 60 cm) circulars and set of 5 dpn in larger size

NOTIONS: 1 button

GAUGE: 22 sts on larger size needles = 4 in (10 cm).

Adjust needle size to obtain correct gauge if necessary.

The vest begins at lower edge and is worked in the round on
a circular needle.

With smaller size circular, CO 92 (100, 108, 120, 128, 136,
144, 152) sts. Join, being careful not to twist cast-on row. Pm
for beginning of rnd.

Work 8 (8, 8, 8, 10, 10, 10, 10) rnds in k1, p1 ribbing.

Change to larger size circular.
Work around in stockinette until body measures 6 (7, 8, 9, 9¾,
10¾, 12¾, 13¾) in [15 (18, 20, 23, 25, 27, 32, 35) cm].
BO 5 sts and work the next 36 (40, 44, 50, 54, 58, 62, 66) sts
back and forth for back from this point on. Place rem sts on
a holder.

BACK
RS: K4, sl 1, k1, psso, k2, sl 1, k1, psso, knit until 10 sts rem,
k2tog, k2, k2tog, k4.
WS: K4, purl until 4 sts rem, k4.
Rep these two rows until 16 (16, 16, 16, 18, 18, 18, 18) sts
rem.
On last row (WS), decrease 0 (0, 0, 2, 2, 2, 2, 2) sts evenly
spaced across = 16 sts rem (all sizes).

On next RS row, K4, sl 1, k1, psso, sl 1, k1, psso, k2tog, k2tog,
k4 = 12 sts rem.
BACK PATTERN:
Row 1: K4, p4, k4.
Row 2: Knit.
Row 3: K4, p4, k4.
Row 4: K5, yo, k1, yo, k1, yo, k5.
Row 5: K4, p7, k4.
Row 6: K5, yo, k1, yo, k3, yo, k1, yo, k5.
Row 7: K4, p11, k4.
Row 8: K5, yo, k3, yo, k3, yo, k3, yo, k5.

Row 9: K4, p15, k4.
Row 10: K5, yo, k13, yo, k5.
Row 11: K4, p17, k4.
Row 12: K5, yo, k4, 7 sts (p1, k1) ribbing, k4, yo, k5.
Row 13: K4, p6, 7 sts (k1, p1) ribbing, p6, k4.
Row 14: K5, yo, k5, BO 7 sts in ribbing, k5, yo, k5.
Now you have two straps, to be worked separately.

Left Strap
WS Row: K4, p4, k3.
RS Row: K3, sl 1, k1, psso, k6.
Rep these 2 rows once more.

STRAP PATTERN
Row 1 (WS): K4, p4, k3.
Row 2: K3, sl 1, k1 psso, k6.
Row 3: K4, p3, k3.
Row 4: K3, sl 1, k1 psso, k5.
Row 5 : K4, p2, k3. Sizes 3-6 (6-9) months: BO in pattern on this row.
Row 6: Knit.
Row 7: K4, p2, k3.
Rep Rows 6-7 0 (0, 1, 2, 3, 4, 5, 6) times and then BO on last row.

Right Strap
WS Row: K3 p4, k4.
RS Row: K5, yo, k1, k2tog, k3.
Rep these 2 rows once more.

STRAP PATTERN
Row 1 (WS): K3, p4, k4.
Row 2: K6, k2tog, k3.
Row 3: K3, p3, k4.
Row 4: K5, k2tog, k3.
Row 5: K3, p2, k4. **Sizes 3-6 (6-9) months:** BO in pattern on this row.
Row 6: Knit.
Row 7: K3, p2, k4.
Rep Rows 6-7 0 (0, 1, 2, 3, 4, 5, 6) times and then BO on last row.

FRONT
With RS facing, BO 9 sts, k4, sl 1, k1, psso, sl 1, k1, psso, knit until 12 sts rem, k2tog, k2tog, k4, BO 4 sts. Cut yarn.

FRONT PATTERN
Row 1 (WS): K4, purl until 4 sts rem, k4.
Row 2 (RS): K4, sl 1, k1, psso, sl 1, k1, psso, knit until 8 sts rem, k2tog, k2tog, k4.
Row 3: K4, purl until 4 sts rem, k4.
Rows 4-5: Work Rows 2-3 once more.

Row 6: K4, sl 1, k1, psso, knit until 6 sts rem, k2tog, k4.
Row 7: K4, purl until 4 sts rem, k4.
Row 8: Knit.
Row 9: K4, purl until 4 sts rem, k4 = 24 (28, 32, 38, 42, 46, 50, 54) sts rem.
Rep Rows 8-9 0 (0, 1, 2, 4, 4, 6, 6) more times.

Now divide front into two halves:
Short Row: K14 (16, 18, 21, 23, 25, 27, 29); turn.
Next Row: K4, p6 (8, 10, 13, 15, 17, 19, 21), k4.
Rep these 2 rows until you have 4 (4, 4, 5, 6, 6, 7, 7) garter ridges on neck placket).

Buttonhole Row (RS): Knit until 3 sts rem, BO 1 st, k2.
On next row, CO 1 st over gap.
Work 3 more rows as for row before buttonhole.

Next Row (WS): BO 4 sts (buttonhole band), k3, p3 (5, 7, 10, 12, 14, 16, 18), k4.

KlompeLompe Spøt, color 4011

All sizes except 3-6 months:
Next Row: Knit until 7 sts rem, k2tog, k2tog, k3.
Next Row: K3, purl until 4 sts rem, k4.
Rep these 2 rows – (0, 1, 2, 3, 4, 5, 6) more times.

All sizes:
Next Row: K5 (5, 5, 6, 6, 6, 6, 6), k2tog, k3.

Sizes 2 (4, 6, 8, 10) years:
Next Row: K3, p3, k4.
Next Row: K5, k2tog, k3.

All sizes:
Rep these 2 rows 4 (4, 5, 5, 6, 6, 7, 8) more times:
Row 1: K3, p2, k4.
Row 2: Knit.
BO on last row.

RIGHT FRONT

CO 4 sts, knit to end of row = 14 (16, 18, 21, 23, 25, 27, 29) sts.

Next Row: K4, p6 (8, 10, 13, 15, 17, 19, 21), k4.
Next Row: Knit.

Rep these 2 rows until you have 6 (6, 6, 7, 8, 8, 9, 9) garter ridges on neck placket).

Next Row (WS): K4, p3 (5, 7, 10, 12, 14, 16, 18), k3, BO 4 sts (button band).

All sizes except 3-6 months:
Next Row: K3, sl 1, k1, psso, sl 1, k1, psso, knit to end of row.
Next Row: K4, purl until 3 sts rem, k3.

Rep these 2 rows – (0, 1, 2, 3, 4, 5, 6) more times.

All sizes:
Next Row: K3, sl 1, k1, psso, knit to end of row.

Sizes 2 (4, 6, 8, 10) years:
Next Row: K4, p3, k3.
Next Row: K3, sl 1, k1, psso, knit to end of row.

All sizes:
Rep these 2 rows 4 (4, 5, 5, 6, 6, 7, 8) times:
Row 1: K4, p2, k3.
Row 2: Knit.
BO on last row.

FINISHING

Seam shoulders with Kitchener st (see page 22).
Weave in all ends neatly on WS.
Sew on button.
Block by covering sweater with a damp towel and leaving it until completely dry or gently steam-press under a damp pressing cloth.

KlompeLompe Tynn merinoull,
Color A: 2652, B: 1013, C: 6521, D: 7251

Dinosaur Cardigan ⟶⟩⟩

Dinosaur Cardigan

Some children are happy with just one type of toy. For Ludvig,
it was dinosaurs. His books all had to be about dinosaurs, the teddy bear in his bed was
tossed out in favor of dinosaur toys, and everything he found in the woods reminded
him of dinosaurs. It was, of course, super great that his
favorite also appeared on his cardigan.

SIZES: 1 (2, 4, 6, 8, 10 years)

FINISHED MEASUREMENTS:
Chest: Approx. 21¾ (22½, 24¾, 28, 29½, 30½) in [55 (57, 63, 71, 75, 77.5) cm]
Total length: Approx. 13 (15, 16½, 18¼, 19½, 20½) in [33 (38, 42, 46.5, 49.5, 52) cm]

YARN: Sandnes Garn KlompeLompe Tynn merinoull (fine merino wool) [CYCA #1—fingering, 100% merino wool, 191 yd (175 m) / 50 g]

YARN COLORS AND AMOUNTS:
Color A (MC): Light Petroleum Blue 6521: 150 (150, 200, 200, 250, 300) g
Color B: Putty 1013: 50 (50, 50, 50, 50, 50) g
Color C: Gray-Brown 2652: 50 (50, 50, 50, 50, 50) g
Color D: Blue-Petroleum 7251: 50 (50, 50, 50, 50, 50) g

NEEDLES: US sizes 1.5 and 2.5 (2.5 and 3 mm): 16 and 24 in (40 and 60 cm) circulars; sets of 5 dpn

NOTIONS: 7 (8, 8, 8, 9, 9) buttons

GAUGE: 27 sts on larger size needles = 4 in (10 cm).

Adjust needle size to obtain correct gauge if necessary.

The cardigan is worked from the top down and, initially, worked back and forth.

With color A (MC) and smaller size circular, CO 91 (95, 101, 101, 109, 109) sts. Work back and forth in k1, p1 ribbing for 1¼ (1¼, 1¼, 1⅜, 1⅜, 1⅜) in [3 (3, 3, 3.5. 3.5, 3.5) cm].

Change to larger size circular and join to work in the round. Knit 1 rnd, ending with CO 7 for steek.

NOTE: Steek sts are not included in stitch counts or on charts. Do not work increases within steek.

Knit 1 rnd, increasing 46 (50, 44, 52, 52, 52) sts evenly spaced around = 137 (145, 145, 153, 161, 161) sts. Now begin pattern following chart.
After completing charted rows, there should be 239 (253, 253, 305, 321, 321) sts.
With MC, knit 0 (4, 3, 5, 8, 8) rnds. Knit next rnd, increasing 8 (6, 26, 0, 0, 12) sts evenly spaced around = 247 (259, 279, 305, 321, 333) sts.
Size 4 years only: Knit 4 rnds.
Sizes 8 (10) years only: Knit 4 (6) rnds.

Sizes 1 (2, 4) years

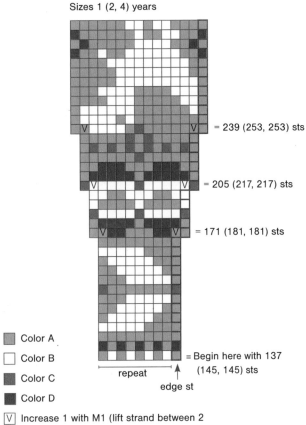

= 239 (253, 253) sts

= 205 (217, 217) sts

= 171 (181, 181) sts

Color A

Color B

Color C

Color D

V Increase 1 with M1 (lift strand between 2
sts and, with color indicated in square, knit
into back loop)

repeat

= Begin here with 137
(145, 145) sts

edge st

Sizes 6 (8, 10) years

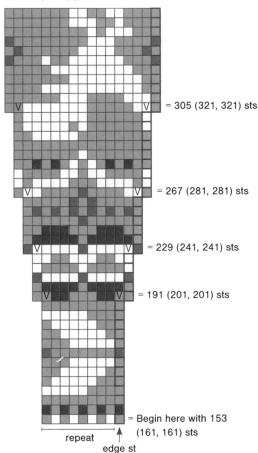

= 305 (321, 321) sts

= 267 (281, 281) sts

= 229 (241, 241) sts

= 191 (201, 201) sts

= Begin here with 153
(161, 161) sts

repeat

edge st

Place sleeve sts on holders as follows:

K33 (34, 38, 43, 46, 47), place next 56 (60, 62, 64, 66, 69)
sts on a holder for sleeve, CO 7 sts for underarm, k69 (71,
79, 91, 97, 101), place next 56 (60, 62, 64, 66, 69) sts on a
holder, CO 7 sts for underarm, k33 (34, 38, 43, 46, 47).

FRONT AND BACK
You should now have 149 (153, 169, 191, 203, 209) sts for
body. Work around in stockinette with MC until piece measures
11¾ (13¾, 15½, 17, 18¼, 19) in [30 (35, 39, 43, 46, 48) cm].
Knit 1 rnd, binding off steek sts.
Change to smaller size circular and work back and forth in

k1, p1 ribbing for 1¼ (1¼, 1¼, 1⅜, 1⅜, 1½) in [3 (3, 3, 3.5.
3.5, 4) cm]. BO in ribbing on last row.

SLEEVES
With larger size dpn, CO 4 sts, k56 (60, 62, 64, 66, 69) held
sts, CO 3 sts.
The sleeve is worked in the round on dpn. The first st should
be marked as the center st of underarm. Always purl marked
st.

When sleeve is ¾ in [2 cm] long, begin shaping sleeve: P1
(marked st), k2tog, knit until 2 sts before marked st, sl 1, k1,
psso.

At back: Color A: 6521, B: 1013, C: 2652, D: 7251
Center: Color A: 2652, B: 1013, C: 6521, D: 7251
In front: Color A: 6033, B: 1013, C: 2652, D: 6061

Decrease the same way every ¾ (¾, ¾, 1, 1, 1¼) in [2 (2, 2, 2.5, 2.5, 3) cm] until 45 (49, 49, 51, 51, 56) sts rem. Continue without further decreasing until sleeve is 7½ (8¾, 9¾, 10¾, 12¼, 13½) in [19 (22, 25, 27, 31, 34) cm] long. Knit 1 rnd, decreasing 1 (1, 1, 1, 1, 0) sts. Change to smaller size dpn and work around in k1, p1 ribbing for 1¼ (1¼, 1¼, 1⅜, 1⅜, 1½) in [3 (3, 3, 3.5. 3.5, 4) cm]. BO in ribbing on last rnd. Make second sleeve the same way.

FINISHING

Machine-stitch two lines of fine sts on each side of center steek st. Carefully cut steek open up center st.
Make buttonhole bands on right side for girl's sweater and on left for boy's.
Button band: With MC and smaller size needle, pick up and knit approx. 3 sts for every 4 rows up front edge.

Work 8 rows in k1, p1 ribbing. BO in ribbing, making sure bind-off is not too tight.
Buttonhole band: Work as for button band, *but*, on Row 3: make 7 (8, 8, 8, 9, 9) buttonholes evenly spaced. BO 2 sts for each buttonhole and CO 2 sts over each gap on next row.
Fold steek edges to WS and sew down with fine stitches. If it is too difficult to stitch down edges neatly, you can knit a facing. Pick up and knit the same number of sts along front edge as for band. Work back and forth in stockinette until facing covers cut edge. BO and sew down facing using MC so stitching won't show on RS.

Weave in all ends neatly on WS.
Sew on buttons.
Block by covering sweater with a damp towel and leaving it until completely dry.

Dinosaur Cap

A sturdy summer cap knitted in fine yarn and just right for all the girls and boys who love dinosaurs.

SIZES: 6-12 months (1-2, 3-6, 8-12 years)

YARN: Sandnes Garn KlompeLompe Tynn merinoull (fine merino wool) [CYCA #1—fingering, 100% merino wool, 191 yd (175 m) / 50 g]

YARN COLORS AND AMOUNTS:
Color A: Dark Gray-Blue 6061: 50 (50, 50, 50) g
Color B: Putty 1013: 50 (50, 50, 50) g

NEEDLES: US sizes 1.5 and 2.5 (2.5 and 3 mm): 16 in (40 cm) circulars and sets of 5 dpn or 32 in (80 cm) magic loop circular

GAUGE: 27 sts on larger size needles = 4 in (10 cm).

Adjust needle size to obtain correct gauge if necessary.

With color A and smaller size circular or dpn, CO 92 (100, 108, 116) sts. Join, being careful not to twist cast-on row; pm for beginning of rnd. Work around in k1, p1 ribbing for 1¼ (1¼, 1¼, 1¼) in [3 (3, 3, 3) cm].

Change to larger size circular. Knit 1 rnd, increasing 12 sts evenly spaced around = 104 (112, 120, 128) sts.

Pm as follows: k26 (30, 34, 38), pm, k16, pm, knit to end of rnd.

Now set up pattern:
Rnd 1: *K1 with color A, k1 with color B*; rep * to * around except for the 16 sts between markers—knit these 16 sts following chart.
Rnd 2: *K1 with color B, k1 with color A*; rep * to * around except for the 16 sts between markers—knit these 16 sts following chart.
Rep Rnds 1-2 until charted rows have been completed.

Continue with color A only in stockinette until cap measures approx. 4¼ (5¼, 6¼, 7) in [11 (13, 16, 18) cm].

Shape crown as follows:
NOTE: Change to dpn when sts no longer fit around circular.
Decrease Rnd 1: *K6, k2tog*; rep * to * around = 91 (98, 105, 112) sts rem.
Knit 3 rnds.

Decrease Rnd 2: *K5, k2tog*; rep * to * around = 78 (84, 90, 96) sts rem.
Knit 2 rnds.

Decrease Rnd 3: *K4, k2tog*; rep * to * around = 65 (70, 75, 80) sts rem.
Knit 2 rnds.

Decrease Rnd 4: *K3, k2tog*; rep * to * around = 52 (56, 60, 64) sts rem.
Knit 2 rnds.

Decrease Rnd 5: *K6, k2tog*; rep * to * around, ending with k4 (0, 4, 0) = 46 (49, 53, 56) sts rem.
Knit 2 rnds.

Decrease Rnd 6: *K5, k2tog*; rep * to * around, ending with k4 (0, 4, 0) = 40 (42, 46, 48) sts rem.
Knit 1 rnd.

Decrease Rnd 7: *K4, k2tog*; rep * to * around, ending with k4 (0, 4, 0) = 34 (35, 39, 40) sts rem.
Knit 1 rnd.

Decrease Rnd 8: *K3, k2tog*; rep * to * around, ending with k4 (0, 4, 0) = 28 (28, 32, 32) sts rem.
Knit 1 rnd.

Decrease Rnd 9: *K2, k2tog*; rep * to * around = 21 (21, 24, 24) sts rem.
Knit 1 rnd.

Last Decrease Rnd: K2tog around, ending with k1 (1, 0, 0).

Cut yarn and draw end through rem sts; tighten.

FINISHING
Weave in all ends neatly on WS.
Block by covering cap with a damp towel and leaving until completely dry.

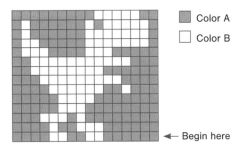

■ Color A
□ Color B

← Begin here

Henry Pullover: KlompeLompe Tynn
merinoull, color 6033

Dinosaur Headband

"It's a T. rex, mama!"

SIZES: 6-12 months (1-2, 3-6, 8-12 years)
YARN: Sandnes Garn KlompeLompe Tynn merinoull (fine merino wool) [CYCA #1—fingering, 100% merino wool, 191 yd (175 m) / 50 g]
YARN COLORS AND AMOUNTS:
Color A: Blue-Green 6571: 50 (50, 50, 50) g
Color B: ??3081: 50 (50, 50, 50) g
NEEDLES: US sizes 1.5 and 2.5 (2.5 and 3 mm): 16 in (40 cm) circulars; set of 5 dpn in larger size
GAUGE: 27 sts on larger size needles = 4 in (10 cm).
Adjust needle size to obtain correct gauge if necessary.

With color A and smaller size circular, CO 92 (100, 108, 116) sts. Join, being careful not to twist cast-on row; pm for beginning of rnd. Work around in k1, p1 ribbing for 1¼ (1¼, 1¼, 1¼) in [3 (3, 3, 3) cm].

Change to larger size circular. Knit 1 rnd, increasing 12 sts evenly spaced around = 104 (112, 120, 128) sts.

Pm as follows: k26 (30, 34, 38), pm, k16, pm, knit to end of rnd.
Now knit 1 (2, 4, 4) rnds.

Continue:
Rnd 1: *K1 with color A, k1 with color B*; rep * to * around except for the 16 sts between markers – knit these 16 sts following chart.
Rnd 2: *K1 with color B, k1 with color A*; rep * to * around except for the 16 sts between markers – knit these 16 sts following chart.
Rep Rnds 1-2 until charted rows have been completed.

Continue with color A only for 1 (2, 4, 4) rnds.

Knit 1 rnd decreasing 12 sts evenly spaced around = 92 (100, 108, 116) sts rem.

Change to smaller size circular and work around in k1, p1 ribbing for 1¼ (1¼, 1¼, 1¼) in [3 (3, 3, 3) cm].
BO loosely in ribbing on last rnd.

FINISHING
Weave in all ends neatly on WS.
Block by covering headband with a damp towel and leaving until completely dry.

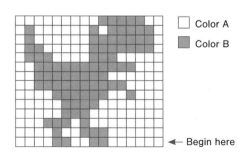

☐ Color A
▨ Color B

← Begin here

Eivind Sweater-Jacket:
KlompeLompe merinoull, color 7251,
Blue-Petroleum

Pocket Rompers

Delightful and simple rompers with fun pocket details.
You can either make the pockets with a lightweight fabric
or knit them in a contrast color.

SIZES: 0-2 (3, 6 months, 1, 2, 4 years)

FINISHED MEASUREMENTS:
Chest: Approx. 12¾ (14½, 16¼, 18¼, 19¾, 21¼) in [32 (37, 41, 46, 50, 54) cm]
Total length: Approx. 13½ (14¼, 15¾, 17, 19, 21¼) in [34 (36, 40, 43, 48, 54) cm]

YARN: Sandnes Garn Duo (fine merino wool) [CYCA #3 – DK, light worsted, 55% merino wool, 45% cotton, 126 yd (115 m) / 50 g]

YARN COLORS AND AMOUNTS:
Color 2650: 150 (150, 150, 150, 200, 250) g + (optional) 50 g contrast color

NEEDLES:

US size 2.5 (3 mm): 16 in (40 cm) or optional 32 in (80) cm circular for magic loop; set of 5 dpn;

US size 4 (3.5 mm): 16 or 24 in [40 or 60 cm] circular

NOTIONS: optional fabric for pocket linings

GAUGE: 22 sts on larger size needles = 4 in (10 cm).

Adjust needle size to obtain correct gauge if necessary.

The rompers begin with a doubled bib at the back, worked back and forth on a circular.

BIB
With smaller size circular, CO 28 (32, 36, 40, 42, 44) sts. Work back and forth in stockinette for 2 (2½, 2½, 2¾, 3¼, 3½) in [5 (6, 6, 7, 8, 9) cm]. The next row = WS; knit 1 row (foldline). Work in stockinette for another 2 (2½, 2½, 2¾, 3¼, 3½) in [5 (6, 6, 7, 8, 9) cm].

Place sts on a holder or spare needle. Fold and seam sides.

DOUBLE STRAPS
Right Strap:
With RS facing and with dpn, pick up and knit 6 sts along top of bib (beginning at fold) and CO 6 sts = 12 sts. Divide sts onto dpn (or use magic loop) and join.

NOTE:
We recommend you use magic loop if you know the technique. That way, you can pick up and knit 6 sts on the back instead of casting on 6 sts on the needles. See a video for magic loop at klompelompe.no

Knit 6 (6, 7, 7, 8, 8) rnds in stockinette.
Next, Increase, Rnd: K1, M1 (lift strand between 2 sts and knit into back loop), knit until 1 st rem, M1, k1.
Continue in stockinette, increasing on every 4th rnd until there are 20 (24, 28, 32, 34, 36) sts.
Work around in stockinette without increasing for 2 (2½, 2½, 2¾, 3¼, 3½) in [5 (6, 6, 7, 8, 9) cm].
Place the first 10 (12, 14, 16, 17, 18) sts on one needle and the next 10 (12, 14, 16, 17, 18) sts on another needle. Use a third needle to join the two sets of sts (*k2tog with first st of each needle*; rep * to * to end of row) = 10 (12, 14, 16, 17, 18) sts rem. Leave sts on needle.

Color 4344

Left Strap:
With RS facing and with dpn, CO 6 sts, pick up and knit 6 sts at left side of bib = 12 sts. Work as for right strap but, when you've worked 2 (2½, 2½, 2¾, 3¼, 3½) in [5 (6, 6, 7, 8, 9) cm] in stockinette, k10 (12, 14, 16, 17, 18) before you knit the sts on front and back together.

Change to larger size circular and join the pieces as follows:

Beginning on RS, knit right strap, CO 11 (13, 13, 15, 17, 19) sts, knit sts from bib, CO 11 (13, 13, 15, 17, 19) sts, knit sts of left strap. Join to work in the round = 70 (82, 90, 102, 110, 118) sts.

Work 3 rnds with stockinette all around except for the 11 (13, 13, 15, 17, 19) sts on each underarm which are worked in k1, p1 ribbing.

Knit 1 rnd, increasing 28 sts evenly spaced around = 98 (110, 118, 130, 138, 146) sts.

Knit 8 rnds.

Knit 1 rnd, increasing 28 sts evenly spaced around = 126 (138, 146, 158, 166, 174) sts.

Raise back with short rows as follows:
K10; turn, yo, p20. Turn, yo, k25. Turn, yo, p30. Turn, k35. Turn, yo, p40. Turn, yo, k20 (you are now back at beginning of rnd).

From this point on, take all measurements from the shoulder down.

When piece measures 6¼ (6¾, 7, 8, 9½, 11) in [16 (17, 18, 20, 24, 28) cm], work opening for pockets as follows:

K40 (43, 44, 48, 50, 52); turn. P80 (86, 88, 96, 100, 104); turn.
Work back and forth on the 80 (86, 88, 96, 100, 104) sts for back and place rem 46 (52, 58, 62, 66, 70) sts for front on a holder.

Work back sts for approx. 3¼ (3¼, 3¼, 3½, 3½, 4) in [8 (8, 8, 9, 9, 10) cm], ending with a WS row. K40 (43, 44, 48, 50, 52) (you are now at center back). Leave sts on holder.
Work the same way as for back on the held 46 (52, 58, 62, 66, 70) sts, but, begin by working on all the sts and end with a WS row.

Begin again at center back, working around until piece measures 11¾ (12¾, 13½, 15, 16½, 19) in [30 (32, 34, 38, 42, 48) cm].

Cut yarn and place the last 10 (10, 10, 14, 16, 18) sts on left needle. Work the last 20 (20, 20, 28, 32, 36) sts (back) back and forth (place rem sts on a holder) as follows:

Work 2 rows in stockinette. On next row (RS): K2tog, knit until 2 sts rem, sl 1, k1, psso. Purl on WS.

Decrease the same way on RS rows until 8 (8, 8, 12, 14, 18) sts rem on needle. Work 6 rows in stockinette, binding off on last row.

Place the 45 (51, 55, 53, 53, 53) sts at each side onto holders and work the 16 (16, 16, 24, 28, 32) sts at front separately. Decrease as for back until 8 (8, 8, 12, 14, 18) sts rem on needle. Work 10 rows in stockinette. BO.

Join front and back with Kitchener st (see page 22).

EDGING AROUND LEGS
Change to smaller size dpn, Pick up and knit sts beginning at crotch. Pick up and knit approx. 16 (16, 16, 18, 18, 20) sts, knit held sts, and pick up and knit 16 (16, 16, 18, 18, 20) sts = 77 (83, 87, 89, 89, 93) sts total.

Decrease as follows:
Sl 1, k1, psso, sl 1, k1, psso, knit until 4 sts before marker, k2tog, k2tog; rep * to *.

Rep decrease rnd.

On next rnd, BO knitwise.

Seam lower edge of pocket and, with color A, tack each pocket to romper at a couple of points.

FINISHING
Sew on back of bib; fold lower edge and sew down with MC. Weave in all ends neatly on WS.

Make ties for back:
Thread a strand of yarn into one side of back opening. Twist the strand into a cord while it is attached to the rompers. Knot one end. Make another cord the same way on other side. On the largest sizes, you might want to make one more cord to attach in middle of back opening.

Alternately, you can sew a fabric tie.

Block by covering rompers with a damp towel and leaving until completely dry or gently steam-press under a damp pressing cloth.

SEWN POCKETS
Use the templates to draw the pockets on fabric. There is a template for each side (= two pockets which each slant downward. Cut out the fabric, adding a ⅜ in (1 cm) seam allowance all around. Lay 1 piece from template A facing RS to RS with another from template B (so wrong sides face out). Sew along the dotted line and zigzag along outer edges. Fold back the edges of openings and attach pockets to rompers by hand. The pockets should slant downward.

FINISHING
Weave in all ends neatly on WS.

K17 (17, 17, 19, 19, 21), *k2tog* rep * to * 22 (25, 27, 26, 26, 26) times, k16 (16, 16, 18, 18, 20).
Knit 6 rnds (if you want a contrast color at lower edge of leg, work the 7 rnds with color B and use color B for rest of work.

Now you can either sew in pockets or knit them – each method is explained below:

POCKETS
Begin on left side of opening. With smaller size needles, pick up and knit 18 (18, 18, 20, 20, 22) sts on each side = 36 (36, 36, 40, 40, 44) sts.
Pm on each side with 18 (18, 18, 20, 20, 22) sts between each marker.
Knit 3 rnds.

Next Rnd: K1, sl 1, k1, psso, knit until 1 st before marker, M1, k2, M1, knit until 3 sts before marker, k2tog, k1.

Continue in stockinette, working the decrease/increase rnd every 3rd rnd a total of 5 (5, 5, 6, 7, 8) times.

Knit 2 rnds.

A

B

4 in (10 cm) pocket

3½ in (9 cm) pocket

3¼ in (8 cm) pocket

Lace Tights

Delicate tights with a simple lace pattern and a new cast-on
method for fine lacy edgings.

SIZES: 0-2 (3-6, 6-12 months, 2, 4, 6, 8-10 years)

FINISHED MEASUREMENTS:
Waist: Approx. 12¼ (15¼, 17, 20½, 22, 26¾, 28½) in [31
(38.5, 43, 52, 56, 68, 72.5) cm]
Leg length: Approx. 6¾ (8½, 10¼, 12½, 14½, 18, 20) in [17.5
(21.5, 26, 31.5, 37, 45.5, 51) cm]
Sandnes Garn KlompeLompe Tynn merinoull (fine merino
wool) [CYCA #1—fingering, 100% merino wool, 191 yd (175
m) / 50 g]

YARN COLORS AND AMOUNTS:
Color 4331 Soft Purple or 4344 Powder Pink: 50 (100, 100,
150, 150, 200, 200) g

NEEDLES:
US sizes 1.5 and 2.5 (2.5 and 3 mm): 16 in (40 cm) or optional
32 in (80) cm circular for magic loop and set of 5 dpn in larger
size

NOTIONS: Waistband elastic to fit around waist + seam allowance

GAUGE: 27 sts on larger size needles = 4 in (10 cm).

Adjust needle size to obtain correct gauge if necessary.

Knot Cast-on:
Estimate 4 times more yarn than usual for this cast-on.
CO 4 sts. Pass 3rd st over 4th, pass 2nd st over 4th, and,
finally, pass 1st st over 4th = 1 st/knot.

With larger size dpn, CO 15 (18, 18, 21, 21, 24, 24) knots.
Divide sts onto dpn and join. Pm for beginning of rnd.

Knit 1 rnd, *at the same time,* increasing 15 (18, 18, 21, 21, 24,
24) sts evenly spaced around – increase with kf&b in each
knot = 30 (36, 36, 42, 42, 48, 48) sts.

Knit 2 rnds.

LACE PATTERN
Rnd 1: K2, k2tog, yo, *k4, k2tog, yo*; rep * to * until 2 sts rem,
k2.
Rnds 2-5: Knit (= knit 4 rnds).
Rnd 6: K5, k2tog, yo, *k4, k2tog, yo*; rep * to * until 5 sts rem,
k5.
Rnds 7-10: Knit (= knit 4 rnds).
Rep Rows 1-10.

Rep the 10-row pattern up the leg, shaping leg beginning after
2 in (5 cm) as follows:
K1, M1, work around until 1 st rem, M1, k1 (M1 = lift strand
between sts and knit into back loop).
If the increases occur on a lace rnd, you can omit k2tog before
the first lace hole (instead of working increase) = 2 sts increased
= 32 (38, 38, 44, 44, 50, 50) sts.
Increase as est every 1 in (2.5 cm) a total of 3 (4, 4, 5, 6, 7,
8) times = 38 (46, 46, 54, 56, 64, 66) sts,
Now increase every ⅝ in (1.5 cm) 3 (4, 7, 9, 11, 15, 17) times
= 44 (54, 60, 72, 78, 94, 100) sts.
Continue in pattern until leg measures 6¾ (8½, 10¼, 12½,
14½, 18, 20) in [17.5 (21.5, 26, 31.5, 37, 45.5, 51) cm]. Place
leg sts on a holder and work second leg the same way.

Join Legs:
CO 8 sts, knit sts of second leg, CO 8 sts, knit sts of first leg. The rnd begins in the center of the first 8 sts cast on = center back.

Pm on each side of the 8 sts cast on at front and back.
Knit around and decrease 1 st before and after each set of 8 sts as follows:
Knit to marker, sl 1, k1, psso, knit until 2 sts before next marker, k2tog. Rep * to * around = 4 sts decreased. Decrease the same way on every other rnd a total of 5 times.

Take all measurements from beginning of rnd where you cast on between the legs.
Continue as est until piece measures 6 (6¼, 6¼, 6¼, 6¾, 6¾, 7) in [15 (16, 16, 16, 17, 17, 18) cm] at center back.

Raise back with short rows as follows, and, when you come to a yarnover, work it tog with next st.
K20; turn, yo, p40. Turn, yo, k35. Turn, yo, p30. Turn, k25. Turn, yo, p20. Turn, yo, knit to beginning of rnd) .

Change to smaller size circular. Knit 5 rnds, purl 1 rnd, knit 5 rnds, binding off on last rnd.

FINISHING
Seam short ends of waistband elastic. Fold down waistband at purl rnd and insert elastic. Sew down casing on WS.
Seam crotch.

Weave in all ends neatly on WS.
Block by covering leggings with a damp towel and leaving until completely dry or gently steam-press under a damp pressing cloth.

Little Deer Bonnet

The sweetest bonnet of the summer with a fine-textured pattern and pretty ears. The cap is quick to knit and is, therefore, a perfect and impressive baby gift.

SIZES: 0 (1-3, 3-6, 6-12, 18-24) months

YARN: Sandnes Garn KlompeLompe merinoull [CYCA #3 – DK, light worsted, 100% merino wool, 114 yd (104 m) / 50 g]

YARN COLORS AND AMOUNTS:
Powder Rose 4032: 50 (100, 100, 100, 100) g

NEEDLES: US sizes 2.5 and 4 (3 and 3.5 mm): 16 in (40 cm) circulars or 32 in (80 cm) circular for magic loop (see video on technique at KlompeLompe.no); sets of 5 dpn

GAUGE: 22 sts on larger size needles = 4 in (10 cm).

Adjust needle size to obtain correct gauge if necessary.

STITCHES AND TECHNIQUES

Elongated knit stitch (ek): knit 1 between stitches a k2tog and k2tog tbl st 2 rounds below, k1, pulling loop up with right needle tip to elongate it. Work the next ek in same hole. See video at klompelompe.no.

With smaller size circular, CO 73 (73, 81, 81, 89) sts. Work back and forth in k1, p1 ribbing for 6 (6, 6, 6, 6) rows.

Chane to larger size needle.
Next Row (RS): Knit, decreasing 1 st at center of row.
Purl 1 row.

BEGIN WITH TEXTURE PATTERN

Row 1 (RS): K2, *k2tog, k2tog tbl, k4*; rep * to * until 6 sts rem, k2tog, k2tog tbl, k2.
Row 2: Purl.
Row 3: K2, *1 ek, k2, 1 ek, k4*; rep * to * until 4 sts rem, 1 ek, k2, 1 ek, k2.
Row 4: Purl.
Row 5: Knit.
Row 6: Purl.
Row 7: K6, *k2tog, k2tog tbl, k4*; rep * to * until 2 sts rem, k2.
Row 8: Purl.
Row 9: K6, *1 ek, k2, 1 ek, k4*; rep * to * until 2 sts rem, k2.
Row 10: Purl.
Row 11: Knit.
Row 12: Purl.

Continue in Texture pattern until piece measures approx. 3¼ (4, 4¾, 4¾, 5½) in [8 (10, 12, 12, 14) cm] and you've just worked either Row 6 or 12 in pattern. Now begin working in garter st on the center 16 (16, 20, 20, 22) sts. You can either bind off rem sts or place them on holders. Later, you will sew these sts to the sides of the garter st sections and you can decide whether you want to seam with mattress or Kitchener st.

Color 1013

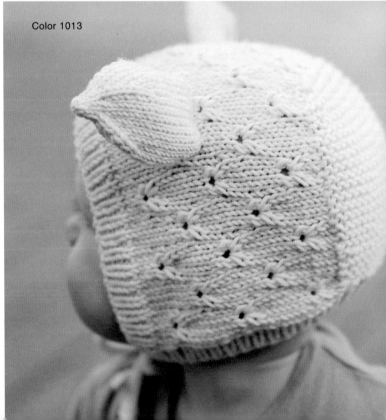

GARTER STITCH PANEL

The first row is on WS.

Knit 3 rows in garter st (knit on RS and knit on WS).

On next (RS) row, increase with M1 as follows:

K1, M1, knit until 1 st rem, M1, k1.

Increase the same way on every 4th row a total of 3 times. Continue in garter st without increasing until garter st panel is 1½ in (4 cm) shorter than length as cap (= length as the sides it will be sewn to).

Decrease on next (RS) row: K2tog, knit until 2 sts rem, k2tog. Decrease the same way on every 4th row a total of 3 times. Continue in garter st until garter st panel is same length as cap (= same length as the sides it will be sewn to).

Place sts on holder. Sew sides of garter st panel to rest of cap.

RIBBING AROUND NECK

With smaller size needle, pick up and knit 3 sts for every 4 rows across side of neck.

Work across garter panel with k2tog. Pick up and knit 3 sts for every 4 rows across opposite side of neck. Work 6 rows back and forth in k1, p1 ribbing. On last row, BO all sts except for the first 3 and last 3 sts. Use these sts to make two I-cords about 7 in (18 cm) long. (For more on I-cord instructions, see video at klompelompe.no).

I-CORD: With dpn, *knit across row; slide sts back to end of needle. Bring yarn across WS, tug yarn slightly, and rep from * until cord is desired length. Cut yarn and draw end through rem sts; tighten and hide end in cord.

EARS

Work with smaller size dpn or long magic loop circular to work in the round.

CO 28 (28, 32, 32, 32) sts. Divide sts onto dpn or magic loop circular and join. Knit around in stockinette for 1¼ (1¼, 1½, 1½, 1½) in [3 (3, 4, 4, 4) cm].

Sizes 3-6 (6-12, 18-24) months: *K6, k2tog*; rep * to * around. Knit 1 rnd.

All sizes:

Decrease Rnd 1: *K5, k2tog*; rep * to * around.
Knit 1 rnd.

Decrease Rnd 2: *K4, k2tog*; rep * to * around.
Knit 1 rnd.

Decrease Rnd 3: *K3, k2tog*; rep * to * around.

Decrease Rnd 4: (K2tog) around.
Knit 3 rnds.

FINISHING

Cut yarn. Draw end through rem sts and tighten. Make second ear the same way.

Fold each ear lengthwise, overlapping sides by ⅜ in (1 cm), and sew together at base. Sew ears to cap, spaced about 3 (3, 3¼, 3¼, 3½) in [7.5 (7.5, 8, 8, 9) cm] apart from each other and approx. 2½ in (6.5 cm) up from ribbing around face.

Weave in all ends neatly on WS. Lay a damp towel over cap and leave until dry or gently steam-press cap under a damp pressing cloth.

Tilda Dress-Leotard

A pretty and detailed dress with a practical leotard
underlayer for the youngest girls.

SIZES: 0-1 (3, 6, 9, 12, 18, 24) months

FINISHED MEASUREMENTS:

Chest: Approx. 16¼ (17½, 18¼, 18¾, 19¾, 20½, 21¾) in
[41.5 (44.5, 46, 47.5, 50, 52, 55) cm]

Length to lower edge of dress: Approx. 10¼ (11½, 12¼, 13,
14¼, 15, 15½) in [26 (29, 31, 33, 36, 38, 39) cm]

YARN: Sandnes Garn KlompeLompe Tynn merinoull (fine merino
wool) [CYCA #1—fingering, 100% merino wool, 191 yd (175
m) / 50 g]

YARN COLORS AND AMOUNTS:

Color 4032 Powder Rose: 150 (150, 150, 200, 200, 200, 250) g

NEEDLES:

US sizes 1.5 and 2.5 (2.5 and 3 mm): 16 and 24 in (40 and
60 cm) and sets of 5 dpn

CROCHET HOOK: US size D-3 (3 mm)

NOTIONS: 5 buttons

GAUGE: 27 sts on larger size needles = 4 in (10 cm).

Adjust needle size to obtain correct gauge if necessary.

STITCHES AND TECHNIQUES

SEED STITCH

Row 1: *K1, p1*; rep * to * across.

All Subsequent Rows: Work purl over knit and knit over purl.

The dress is worked top down and is initially worked back and
forth.

With smaller size circular, CO 64 (68, 68, 72, 76, 80, 84) sts.
Work 4 rows in seed st.
Change to larger size circular.
Knit 1 row and pm as follows:
K11 (12, 12, 13, 14, 15, 16), pm, k10 (sleeve sts), pm, k22
(24, 24, 26, 28, 30, 32), pm, k10 (sleeve sts), pm, k11 (12,
12, 13, 14, 15, 16).
Purl 1 row.

Continue in stockinette, increasing at markers on every RS
row:
*Knit until 1 st before marker, knit into st below (RLI), k1 on
needle. Knit into st below st after marker.* Rep * to * across
= 8 sts increased total.

Increase a total of 9 (9, 9, 10, 10, 10, 10) times and then join
to work in the round. Continue increasing as est on every
other rnd. After increasing a total of 13 (14, 15, 15, 16, 16,
17) times, knit next rnd, slipping sleeve sts to holders; CO 8
sts at each underarm = 112 (120, 124, 128, 136, 140, 148)
sts.

Knit 5 (5, 5, 6, 6, 8, 8) rnds. Purl 1 rnd, knit 1 rnd. Knit next
rnd increasing 10 sts evenly spaced around = 122 (130, 134,
138, 146, 150, 158) sts.

Raise back with short rows as follows, and, when you come
to a yarnover, work it tog with next st.

Sizes 0-1 (3, 6, 9) months:

K15; turn, yo, p30. Turn, yo, k40. Turn, yo, p50. Turn, k25 (you
should now be back to beginning of rnd) .

Sizes 12 (18, 24) months:

K15; turn, yo, p30. Turn, yo, k40. Turn, yo, p50. Turn, k60. Turn, yo, p70. Turn, yo, k35 (you should now be back to beginning of rnd).

Continue in stockinette until piece measures 10¼ (11½, 12¼, 13, 14¼, 15, 15½) in [26 (29, 31, 33, 36, 38, 39) cm] down front.

Cut yarn. Slip next 27 (29, 30, 32, 34, 35, 37) sts to right needle. Re-attach yarn to begin knitting here.

BO 19 (21, 21, 21, 21, 22, 24) sts, k30 (30, 32, 32, 36, 36, 36) sts, BO 19 (21, 21, 21, 21, 22, 24) sts. Now work back separately, back and forth = 54 (58, 60, 64, 68, 70, 74) sts. The first row is on RS.

On each RS row: Decrease 1 st on each side with k2tog with first 2 sts and k2tog with last 2 sts. Decrease the same way until 22 (22, 24, 24, 26, 26, 26) sts rem. Place sts on a holder while you knit front.

FRONT

Work as for back on the 30 (30, 32, 32, 36, 36, 36) sts, decreasing until 22 (22, 24, 24, 26, 26, 26) sts rem. Continue without decreasing until front is ¾ (¾, ¾, ¾, ¾, 1¼, 1¼) in [2 (2, 2, 2, 2, 3, 3) cm] shorter than back. Place sts on holder while you knit ribbing around legs.

With smaller size needle, pick up and knit 3 sts for every 4 sts around leg. Work 6 rows k1, p1 ribbing, binding off in ribbing on last row. Work ribbing on second leg the same way.

BUTTON/BUTTONHOLE BANDS AT CROTCH

Button Band on Back: With smaller size needles, pick up and knit 4 sts at end of ribbing around leg, knit held sts, pick up and knit 4 sts on other side of ribbing. Work 6 rows in k1, p1 ribbing.

Buttonhole Band on Front: Work as for back band, but, make 4 buttonholes evenly spaced on 2nd row: BO 2 sts for each buttonhole and CO 2 sts over each gap on 3rd row.

SLEEVES

Place the 36 (38, 40, 40, 42, 42, 44) held sts of one sleeve on larger size needle. Work back and forth, beginning on RS. Knit until 2 sts rem; turn, sl 1, purl until 2 sts rem turn. Sl 1, knit until 4 sts rem; turn. Sl 1, purl until 4 sts rem; turn. Sl 1,

knit to end of row.

Knit 1 row on WS.

Next Row: K14 (14, 15, 15, 14, 14, 15), *k2tog*; rep * to * 4 (5, 5, 5, 7, 7, 7) times, k14 (14, 15, 15, 14, 14, 15).

Knit 3 rows, binding off on last row. Sew edges to dress. Make second sleeve the same way.

Crochet a button loop on one side of back neck opening: ch 5 and attach with 1 sl st. Sew a button to opposite side.

Weave in all ends neatly on WS. Sew on 4 buttons to lower edge of back.

SKIRT

With larger size circular, pick up and knit sts in the purl rnd at middle of body. Pick up approx. 112 (120, 124, 128, 136, 140, 148) sts on lower side of purl rnd. Turn and knit 1 rnd. Knit next rnd, *at the same time*, increasing 8 (8, 4, 8, 8, 12, 12) sts evenly spaced around = 120 (128, 128, 136, 144, 152, 160) sts.

Knit 0 (0, 3, 3, 3, 5, 8) rnds.

Knit 0 (0, 1, 1, 1, 1, 1) rnd, *at the same time*, increasing 16 sts evenly spaced around = – (–, 144, 152, 160, 168, 176) sts.

Knit 0 (0, 2, 8, 10, 12, 14) rnds.

Knit 0 (0, 0, 1, 1, 1, 1) rnd, *at the same time*, increasing 16 sts evenly spaced around = – (–, –, 168, 176, 184, 192) sts.

Knit 0 (0, 0, 2, 4, 6, 10) rnds.

Now work charted lace pattern. Except for size 0-1 months, work part A 2 times.

After completing charted rows, BO using I-cord BO (see video at klompelompe.no). CO 3 sts on a dpn. Slide sts to left needle. *K2, k2tog tbl. Slide the 3 sts on right needle to left needle.* Rep * to * until all sts are bound off. Seam ends of I-cord.

FINISHING

Weave in all ends neatly on WS. Lay a damp towel over dress and leave until dry or gently steam-press under a damp pressing cloth.

TIPS

If you find it difficult to work a double yarnover at the edge, you can shift the first yarnover on this rnd to the beginning of the next rnd.

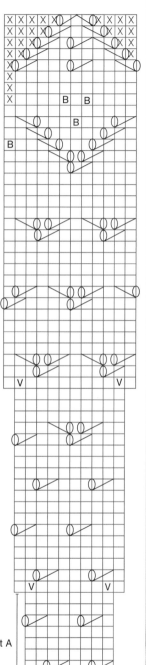

part A

B	Bobble = *K1, yo, k1* in next st; turn. P3; turn. K3; turn.
□	knit
X	purl
◿◺	sl 1, k2tog, psso
◿	k2tog
◺	sl 1, k1, psso
◫	1 yo between 2 sts
V	1 yarnover between 2 sts increase here with M1

Vaja Tunic ———————→ ≫

Vaja Tunic

A charming twist: a sewn fabric skirt at lower edge. Combine the yarn with your favorite fabric. If you don't like to sew, you can make this as a top without the fabric frill.

SIZES: 0-2 (3, 6-9 months, 1, 2, 4, 6 years)

FINISHED MEASUREMENTS:
Chest: Approx. 19¼ (20, 22¾, 24, 26½, 28¼, 29¾) in [49 (51, 58, 61, 67, 72, 75.5) cm]
Length, not including fabric skirt: Approx. 9 (10¼, 11½, 12¾, 13¾, 15, 16½) in [23 (26, 29, 32, 35, 38, 42) cm]

YARN: Sandnes Garn KlompeLompe Spøt [CYCA #3 – DK, light worsted, 40% merino wool, 40% alpaca, 20% nylon, 147 yd (134 m) / 50 g]

YARN COLORS AND AMOUNTS:
Color 6871: 100 (100, 100, 100, 150, 150, 200) g

NEEDLES:
US sizes 2.5 and 4 (3 and 3.5 mm): 16 in (40 cm)

CROCHET HOOK: US size E-4 (3.5 mm)

NOTIONS: 1 button; fabric 4¾ (5½, 6¼, 6¾, 7½, 8, 8¼) in [12 (14, 16, 17, 19, 20, 21) cm] high and approx. 3 times the circumference of lower edge of tunic + seam and hem allowances; sewing thread to match yarn color.

GAUGE: 22 sts on larger size needles = 4 in (10 cm).

Adjust needle size to obtain correct gauge if necessary.

The tunic is worked top down and is initially worked back and forth on a circular needle.

With smaller size circular, CO 66 (66, 74, 74, 78, 80, 80) sts. Knit 3 rows in garter st. The first row = WS. Change to larger size circular. Knit next row, placing markers:

K11 (11, 13, 13, 14, 14, 14), M1, k1 (pm for marked st), M1, k8 (sleeve sts), M1, k1 (pm for marked st), M1, k24 (24, 28, 28, 30, 32, 32), M1, k1 (pm for marked st), M1, k8 (marked sts), M1, k1 (sleeve sts), M1, k11 (11, 13, 13, 14, 14, 14).
All increases are worked with M1 = lift strand between 2 sts and knit into back loop.

Continue in stockinette (= knit on RS and purl on WS), increasing on RS rows.

After increasing 10 (10, 10, 11, 12, 12, 12) times, CO 2 sts at end of row and join to knit in the round. Increase on every other rnd.

After increasing a total of 12 (13, 15, 17, 19, 21, 23) times, there are 164 (172, 196, 212, 232, 250, 266) sts.

On next rnd, decrease away the 4 marked sts. Place the 32 (34, 38, 42, 46, 50, 54) sts of each sleeve on holders and CO 6 sts for each underarm = 108 (112, 128, 136, 148, 158, 166) sts rem. Always purl the st before and after the 6 underarm sts as marked sts = 4 marked sts.

Knit the 6 underarm sts, but, on every 8th rnd, slip these 6 sts onto a dpn and wrap the yarn clockwise around all the sts two times. Knit the 6 sts.

Work around in stockinette for 1¼ in (3 cm). On next rnd, increase as follows: Knit until 1 st before marked st, M1, knit until 1 st after next marked st, M1. Rep the 2 increases at next underarm = 4 increases on round.

Increase the same way every 1 in (2.5 cm) a total of 4 (5, 6, 7, 7, 8, 8) times = 124 (132, 152, 164, 176, 190, 198) sts, Continue until top measures 8¾ (9¾, 11½, 12¼, 13, 14¼, 15¾) in [22 (25, 29, 31, 33, 36, 40) cm] . Change to smaller needle. Purl 1 rnd, knit 8 rnds, binding off on last rnd.

SLEEVES (make both alike)

Work smaller size circular, work back and forth on the 32 (34, 38, 42, 46, 50, 54) sleeve sts. The first row is the RS. Purl 1 row on RS. Work 8 rows in stockinette (= purl on WS and knit on RS). BO on last row.

Button loop: With crochet hook, ch 5 at top of neck opening on left side and attach with 1 sl st. Sew button on right side. Make bobbles on rolled lower edges: Ch 4 and attach through the work directly over the purl rnd with 1 sc. There should be 4 sts in each bobble (see photos below).

FINISHING

Weave in all ends neatly on WS.
Lay a damp towel over dress and leave until dry or gently steam-press under a damp pressing cloth.

SKIRT

Measure the lower edge of tunic. Cut fabric 4¾ (5½, 6¼, 6¾, 7½, 8, 8¼) in [12 (14, 16, 17, 19, 20, 21) cm] high and approx. 3 times the circumference of lower edge of tunic. Zigzag or use overlock around all edges. Seam short ends.

Fold up the lower edge about ⅜ in (1 cm) and iron it down with a steam iron for hem. Sew a simple hem at lower edge.

Now gather the upper edge. Sew two lines of long basting stitches, leaving thread ends. Pull on pairs of ends to gather fabric to match circumference of tunic lower edge. Pin fabric to top and sew it on with two rows of stitching (make sure to use sewing thread matching yarn color).

Back of tunic
Color 4321

Henry Pullover

Some pullovers just look great on everyone. A simple and straightforward knitting project that anyone can make. Notice the button details on one shoulder.

SIZES: 6 months (1, 2, 4, 6, 8, 10 years)

FINISHED MEASUREMENTS:
Chest: Approx. 22¾ (24½, 26¾, 29¼, 29¾, 30¼, 31½) in [58 (62, 68, 74, 75.5, 77, 80) cm]
Total length: Approx. 13¾ (15½, 17¼, 18½, 20½, 21¾, 23¾) in [35 (39, 44, 47, 52, 55.5, 60) cm]

YARN: Sandnes Garn KlompeLompe Tynn merinoull (fine merino wool) [CYCA #1—fingering, 100% merino wool, 191 yd (175 m) / 50 g]

YARN COLORS AND AMOUNTS:
Blue-Green 6571: 100 (150, 200, 200, 250, 250, 300) g

NEEDLES: US sizes 1.5 and 2.5 (2.5 and 3 mm): 16 and 24 in (40 and 60 cm) circulars; sets of 5 dpn

NOTIONS: 2 (2, 2, 2, 2, 2, 2) buttons

GAUGE: 27 sts on larger size needles = 4 in (10 cm).

Adjust needle size to obtain correct gauge if necessary.

The pullover is worked from the bottom up.

With smaller size circular, CO 156 (168, 184, 200, 204, 208, 216) sts. Join, being careful not to twist cast-on row; pm for beginning of rnd. Work around in k1, p1 ribbing for 1¼ (1¼, 1⅜, 1⅜, 1½, 1½, 1½) in [3 (3, 3.5, 3.5. 4, 4, 4) cm]. Change to larger size circular. The rest of the pullover is worked in stockinette. Continue until body measures 8 (9, 10¼, 11, 12¾, 13¾, 15) in [20 (23, 26, 28, 32, 35, 38) cm]. BO 7 sts at each side for underarms as follows:
BO 7, k7l (77, 85, 93, 95, 97, 101), BO 7, k7l (77, 85, 93, 95, 97, 101).

SLEEVES
With smaller size dpn, CO 46 (48, 50, 50, 56, 56, 60) sts. Divide sts onto dpn and join, Work around in k1, p1 ribbing for 1¼ (1¼, 1⅜, 1⅜, 1½, 1½, 1½) in [3 (3, 3.5, 3.5. 4, 4, 4) cm]. Change to larger size dpn. Work around in stockinette except for the first st of rnd which is always purled = marked st.
When sleeve measures 1½ in (4 cm), increase 1 st (with M1) on each side of marked st. Increase the same way approx. every 1½ (1¾, 1¾, 1⅜, 2, 1¾, 2) in [4 (4.5, 4.5, 3.5, 5, 4.5, 5) cm] until there are 52 (56, 60, 64, 68, 70, 74) sts.
Continue without further shaping until sleeve is 6 (8¼, 10, 11¼, 12¼, 13¾, 15) in [15 (21, 25.5, 28.5, 31, 35, 38) cm] long. On next rnd, BO the first 4 and last 3 sts of rnd for underarm. Set sleeve aside while you knit second sleeve the same way.

YOKE
Arrange sleeves and body on larger size circular, matching underarms = 232 (252, 276, 300, 312, 320, 336) sts total.

Pm at each intersection of body and sleeve for raglan shaping = 4 markers.
Begin rnd for raglan shaping before left sleeve. Decrease for raglan at each marker as follows:
K2tog, knit until 2 sts before next marker, sl 1, k1, psso; rep * to * around = 8 decreases.
Decrease the same way on every other rnd.

When you've worked 10 (12, 15, 17, 18, 19, 21) decrease rnds, make neck opening. Cut yarn.

Slip 12 (12, 10, 10, 12, 12, 12) sts to right needle. The opening will be at the side. Begin working back and forth.

CO 5 new sts onto right needle. Always knit these 5 sts on all rows (= garter st). Also knit the last 5 sts of row in garter st. Otherwise, continue in stockinette. Begin on WS and continue raglan shaping on RS rows.

After working 7 rows and next row is RS, make buttonholes.

K2, BO 2 sts, work to end of row. Work WS row as est and CO 2 sts over gap.

Continue until you've decreased a total of 18 (20, 23, 25, 26, 27, 29) times = 93 (97, 97, 105, 109, 109, 109) sts rem.

NECKBAND: Change to smaller size circular. Continue the 5 first and 5 last sts in garter st. Work rem sts in k1, p1 ribbing for 2 rows. On next row of ribbing, make buttonhole as before. Continue in ribbing until you have worked a total of 8 rows; BO in ribbing on last row.

FINISHING
Weave in all ends neatly on WS. Sew on two buttons.
Lay a damp towel over pullover and leave until dry or gently steam-press under a damp pressing cloth.

Crowberry Cap →→

Crowberry Cap

This is a really fun project with both lace and bobbles.

SIZES: 0-3 (3-6, 6-12 months, 1-2, 3-5 years)

YARN: Sandnes Garn KlompeLompe Tynn merinoull (fine merino wool) [CYCA #1—fingering, 100% merino wool, 191 yd (175 m) / 50 g]

YARN COLORS AND AMOUNTS:
Soft Purple 4331: 50 (50, 50, 50, 50) g

NEEDLES: US sizes 1.5 and 2.5 (2.5 and 3 mm): 16 in (40 cm) circulars; sets of 5 dpn; optional 32 in (80 cm) circular for magic loop

GAUGE: 27 sts on larger size needles = 4 in (10 cm).

Adjust needle size to obtain correct gauge if necessary.

With smaller size dpn, CO 4 sts. Make an I-cord 7 in (18 cm) long.

I-CORD

With dpn, *knit across row; slide sts back to end of needle. Bring yarn across WS, tug yarn slightly, and rep from * until cord is desired length. Cut yarn and draw end through rem sts; tighten and hide end in cord.

Now begin working back and forth in stockinette, increasing for the earflap on every RS row: K1, M1, knit until 1 st rem, M1, k1.

Increase the same way on every RS row until there are 26 (28, 30, 30, 32) sts. Place earflap sts on a holder. Make a second I-cord and earflap the same way.

CO 3 sts, knit sts of first earflap, CO 26 (28, 26, 34, 38) sts, knit sts of second earflap, CO 3 sts = 84 (90, 92, 100, 108) sts. Join and pm for beginning of rnd, which begins at center back.

Work 4 rnds in garter st (= purl 1 rnd, knit 1 rnd). On last rnd (knit), increase (with kf&b) 0 (6, 4, 8, 0) sts evenly spaced round = 84 (96, 96, 108, 108) sts.

Change to larger size circular. Work in pattern following chart. Begin on chart row 13 (7, 1, 19, 13). Work through chart row 24 and then rep whole chart.

After completing chart 1.5 (1.5, 1.5, 2.5, 2.5) times and when you are ready to work row 12, continue as follows:
Rnd 1: *P1, sl 1, k1, psso, k7, k2tog*; rep * to * around.
Rnd 2: *P1, k9*; rep * to * around.
Rnd 3: *P1, sl 1, k1, psso, k5, k2tog*; rep * to * around.
Rnd 4: *P1, k7*; rep * to * around.
Rnd 5: *P1, sl 1, k1, psso, B (bobble), k2, yo, k2tog*; rep * to * around.
Rnd 6: *P1, k6*; rep * to * around
Rnd 7: *P1, sl 1, k1, psso, B, k1, yo, k2tog*; rep * to * around.
Rnd 8: *P1, k5*; rep * to * around.

Rnd 9: *P1, sl 1, k1, psso, k1, k2tog*; rep * to * around.
Rnd 10: *P1, k3*; rep * to * around
Rnd 11: *P1, sl 1, k2tog, psso*; rep * to * around.
Rnd 12: *K2tog*; rep * to * around.

Knit rem sts around for 2½ in (6 cm).
Cut yarn and

FINISHING

Weave in all ends neatly on WS. Make a knot at with the 2½ in (6 cm) tip.
Lay a damp towel over cap and leave until dry.

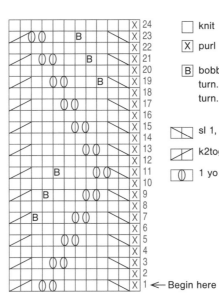

	knit
X	purl
B	bobble = (K1, yo, k1) in next st; turn. P3, turn. K3; turn. P2tog, p1; turn. K2tog.
◹	sl 1, k1, pssor
◿	k2tog
◍◍	1 yo between 2 sts

← Begin here

Wing Cardigan

A round-yoke cardigan with wings on the sleeves. This is a fine choice to wear over a summer dress when it gets a bit chilly.

SIZES: 0-1 (3, 6, 12, 18 months, 2, 4, 6, 8, 10 years)

FINISHED MEASUREMENTS:
Chest: Approx. 17¼ (20, 21½, 21¾, 24½, 24¾, 25½, 26, 26½, 29¼) in [44 (51, 54.5, 55, 62, 63, 65, 66, 67, 74.5) cm]
Length: Approx. 8¾ (9½,10¼, 11, 11¾, 13½, 15, 16½, 18¼, 19¾) in [22 (24, 26, 28, 30, 34, 38, 42, 46, 50) cm]

YARN: Sandnes Garn KlompeLompe Tynn merinoull (fine merino wool) [CYCA #1—fingering, 100% merino wool, 191 yd (175 m) / 50 g]

YARN COLORS AND AMOUNTS:
Dark Gray-Blue 6061: 100 (100, 100, 150, 150, 150, 200, 200, 250, 250) g

NEEDLES: US sizes 1.5 and 2.5 (2.5 and 3 mm): 16 or 24 in (40 or 60 cm) circulars and sets of 5 dpn; 32 in (80 cm) circular for magic loop if preferred

NOTIONS: 3 buttons (all sizes)

GAUGE: 27 sts on larger size needles = 4 in (10 cm).

Adjust needle size to obtain correct gauge if necessary.

The cardigan is worked from the top down, back and forth on a circular.

With smaller size circular, CO 73 (75, 81, 85, 89, 93, 99, 103, 103, 107) sts. Work back and forth in k1, p1 ribbing for 2½ (2½, 2½, 2½, 3¼, 3¼, 3¼, 4, 4, 4) in [6 (6, 6, 6, 8, 8, 8, 10, 10, 10) cm], but, on the 3rd (3rd, 3rd, 3rd, 5th, 5th, 5th, 5th, 5th, 5th) row, make a buttonhole. Work in ribbing until 5 sts rem, BO 2 sts, work 3 sts ribbing. On next row, CO 2 sts over gap. After completing ribbing, work in stockinette (knit on RS, purl on WS) except for the 5 outermost sts on each side which are worked in garter st (knit on all rows). Change to larger size circular. Purl 1 row on WS.

NOTE:
Work total of 3 buttonholes spaced about 1¾ (1¾, 1¾, 2, 2, 2, 2¼, 2¼, 2½, 2½) in 4.5 (4.5, 4.5, 5, 5, 5, 5.5, 5.5, 6, 6) cm] apart.
Buttonhole: Work until 4 sts rem, BO 2 sts, k2. On next row, CO 2 sts over gap.

On next (RS) row, increase (with M1) 20 (20, 21, 22, 24, 24, 30, 30, 30, 30) sts evenly spaced in stockinette section = 93 (95, 102, 107, 113, 117, 129, 133, 133, 137) sts. Work 5 rows in stockinette.
Knit 1 row, increasing 30 sts evenly spaced across stockinette = 123 (125, 132, 137, 143, 147, 159, 163, 163, 167) sts. Work 5 rows in stockinette.
Knit 1 row, increasing 30 sts evenly spaced across stockinette = 153 (155, 162, 167, 173, 177, 189, 193, 193, 197) sts. Work 5 rows in stockinette (except, on sizes 0-1 month and 3 months, work 4 rows in stockinette and knit 1 row on WS).

Knit 1 row, increasing 30 sts evenly spaced across stockinette = 183 (185, 192, 197, 203, 207, 219, 223, 223, 227) sts.
For sizes 0-1 and 3 months: increase with kf&b.

All sizes except 0-1 and 3 months:
Work 5 rows in stockinette, except, on sizes 6 and 12 months, work 4 rows stockinette and knit 1 row on WS.
Knit 1 row, increasing 45 sts evenly spaced across stockinette = – (–, 237, 242, 248, 252, 264, 268, 268, 272) sts.
For sizes 6 and 3 months: increase with kf&b.

All sizes except 0-1, 3, 6, 12 months:
Work 5 rows in stockinette, except, on sizes 18 months, 2, 4, 6, years, work 4 rows stockinette and knit 1 row on WS.
Knit 1 row, increasing 25 sts evenly spaced across stockinette = – (–, –, –, 273, 277, 289, 293, 293, 297) sts.
For sizes 18 months, 2, 4, 6 years: increase with kf&b.

All sizes except 0-1, 3, 6, 12, 18 months, 2, 4, 6 years:
Work 4 rows in stockinette and knit 1 row on WS.
Knit 1 row, increasing, with kf&b, – (–, –, –, –, –, –, –, 20, 30) sts evenly spaced across stockinette = – (–, –, –, –, –, –, –, 313, 327) sts.
Sizes 0-1 and 3 months:
Work 1 (3) rows stockinette.
Work 1 row stockinette, increasing 10 (38) sts evenly spaced across stockinette = 193 (223) sts.

All sizes: Work 3 (3, 3, 5, 3, 5, 7, 9, 3, 7) rows in stockinette.

On next row, divide for sleeves and body:
K27 (32, 35, 35, 39, 40, 41, 42, 45, 48), place 42 (48, 50, 52, 58, 58, 62, 62, 66, 68) sts on holder for sleeve, CO 5 sts for underarm, k55 (63, 67, 68, 79, 81, 83, 85, 91, 95), place 42 (48, 50, 52, 58, 58, 62, 62, 66, 68) sts on holder for sleeve, CO 5 sts for underarm, k27 (32, 35, 35, 39, 40, 41, 42, 45, 48).

Continue in stockinette until body measures 8¾ (9½, 10¼, 11, 11¾, 13½, 15, 16½, 18¼, 19¾) in [22 (24, 26, 28, 30, 34, 38, 42, 46, 50) cm].
On next , RS, row, work eyelets for picot foldline: *k2tog, yo*; rep * to * until 1 (1, 1, 0, 1, 1, 1, 1, 1, 1) sts rem, k1 (1, 1, 0, 1, 1, 1, 1, 1, 1). Work 6 rows in stockinette and BO on last rnd.

SLEEVES (make both alike)
Beginning in middle of 5 sts cast on for underarm, with larger size dpn, pick up and knit 3 sts, k42 (48, 50, 52, 58, 58, 62, 62, 66, 68) held sts, pick up and knit 2 sts on underarm. Divide sts onto 4 dpn.

KNITTING TIP
If you find it difficult to pick up and knit sts, you can cast on the same number of sts and later seam the underarm with Kitchener st (see page 22).

Join to work in the round. The first st is a marked st and is always purled for center of underarm. Work in stockinette for ¾ in (2 cm) and then begin sleeve shaping:
K2tog after marked st and sl 1, k1, psso before marked st. Decrease the same way every 1⅜ (¾, ¾, 1, ¾, 1, 1, 1¼, 1¼, 1¼) in [3.5 (2, 2, 2.5, 2, 2.5, 2.5, 3, 3, 3) cm] until 41 (41, 41, 43, 43, 45, 47, 49, 51, 51) sts rem and sleeve is 4¾ (5½, 6¼, 7, 8, 9, 10¼, 11½, 13, 14¼) in [12 (14, 16, 18, 20, 23, 26, 29, 33, 36) cm] long. Change to smaller size dpn and knit 1 rnd, decreasing to eliminate marked st. Knit 5 rnds.

Next row (RS): Work eyelets for picot foldline: *k2tog, yo*; rep * to * around.
Knit 6 rnds, binding off on last rnd.

WINGS (same on each sleeve)

Pick up sts for the wings under the purl rnd, but on RS. Make sure each wing is centered on the shoulder.

Sizes 0-1, 3, 6, 12, 18 months, 2 years:
With smaller size needle, pick up and knit 31 (33, 35, 35, 37, 39) sts. Knit 1 row on RS and purl 1 row.

Wing Row 1 (RS): K3 (4, 5, 5, 6, 7), M1, *k2, M1*; rep * to * until 2 (3, 4, 4, 5, 6) sts rem, k1 (2, 3, 3, 4, 5); turn.

Wing Row 2: Sl 1, purl until 1 st rem; turn.

Wing Row 3: Sl 1, k3 (4, 5, 5, 6, 7), M1, *k6, M1*; rep * to * 6 times, knit to end of row.

Wing Row 4: Knit.
Change to larger size needle and BO knitwise.

Sizes 4, 6, 8, 10 years:
With smaller size needle, pick up and knit 43 (45, 47, 49) sts. Knit 1 row on RS and purl 1 row.

Wing Row 1 (RS): K4 (5, 5, 6), M1, *k2, M1*; rep * to * until 2 (3, 4, 4) sts rem, k1 (2, 3, 3); turn.

Wing Row 2: Sl 1, purl until 1 st rem; turn.

Wing Row 3: Sl 1, k4 (5, 5, 6), M1, *k3, M1*; rep * to * until 3 (4, 5, 5) sts rem, k1 (2, 3, 3); turn.

Wing Row 4: Sl 1, purl until 2 sts rem; turn.

Wing Row 5: Sl 1, k5 (5, 6, 7), M1, *k6, M1*; rep * to * 6 times, knit to end of row.

Knit 1 row. Change to larger size needle and BO knitwise.

FINISHING

Fold body and sleeve edgings at picot eyelet row and sew down edge on WS.
Weave in all ends neatly on WS.
Sew on 3 buttons.
Block by covering sweater with a damp towel and leaving it until completely dry or gently steam-press under a damp pressing cloth.

Color 1013

Theodor T-shirt

A favorite t-shirt with stripes and button details.

SIZES: 6 (9, 12, 18 months, 2, 4, 6, 8, 10 years)

FINISHED MEASUREMENTS:

Chest: Approx. 19½ (20, 21¼, 21¾, 23¼, 24½, 26½, 29½, 30¾) in [49.5 (51, 54, 55.5, 59, 62, 67.5, 75, 78) cm]

Length: Approx. 12¾ (13½, 14¼, 15½, 16¼, 17, 19¼, 21¼, 22) in [32 (34, 36.5, 39, 41, 43.5, 49, 54, 56) cm]

MATERIALS

YARN: Sandnes Garn KlompeLompe Tynn merinoull (fine merino wool) [CYCA #1—fingering, 100% merino wool, 191 yd (175 m) / 50 g]

YARN COLORS AND AMOUNTS:

Color A: Putty 1013: 50 (50, 100, 100, 100, 100, 100, 100, 150) g

Color B: Dark Gray-Blue 6061: 50 (50, 50, 100, 100, 100, 100, 100, 100) g

NEEDLES: US sizes 1.5 and 2.5 (2.5 and 3 mm): 16 and 24 in (40 and 60 cm) circulars and sets of 5 dpn; 32 in (80 cm) circulars for magic loop if preferred

NOTIONS: 6 (6, 6, 6, 6, 8, 8, 8, 8) buttons

GAUGE: 27 sts on larger size needles = 4 in (10 cm).

Adjust needle size to obtain correct gauge if necessary.

The T-shirt is worked from the bottom up in the round on a circular needle.

With smaller size circular and color A, CO 134 (138, 146, 150, 160, 168, 182, 202, 210) sts. Join, being careful not to twist

cast-on row; pm for beginning of rnd. Work around in k1, p1 ribbing for 1 (1, 1¼, 1¼, 1¼, 1¼, 1¼, 1⅜, 1⅜) in [2.5 (2.5, 3, 3, 3, 3, 3, 3.5, 3.5) cm].

Change to larger size needle.

Change to color B and begin stripe sequence: Work 4 rnds color B, 4 rnds color A.

Continue in stripe pattern until body measures 7½ (8¼, 9, 9¾, 10¼, 11, 12¾, 13¾, 15) in [19 (21, 23, 25, 26, 28, 32, 35, 38) cm] and 1 rnd of a stripe rem.

Next Rnd: BO 8 sts at each side on last stripe rnd.

Set body aside while you knit sleeves.

SLEEVES

With smaller size dpn and color A, CO 48 (48, 50, 50, 52, 54, 64, 66, 70) sts. Divide sts onto dpn and join. Work around in stockinette for ¾ in (2 cm). Purl 1 rnd (foldline). Begin stripe pattern.

Measure 1 (1¼, 1¼, 1⅜, 1⅜, 1½, 2, 2, 2¼) in [2.5 (3, 3, 3.5, 3.5, 4, 5, 5, 5.5) cm] from top down on body to determine which color to begin with after foldline on sleeve. This will help you match sleeves and body when you join the pieces for the yoke.

Change to larger size dpn and work in stripe pattern until sleeve measures 1 (1¼, 1¼, 1⅜, 1⅜, 1½, 2, 2, 2¼) in [2.5 (3, 3, 3.5, 3.5, 4, 5, 5, 5.5) cm] above rnd where you changed needle size. BO 8 sts centered on underarm on the last rnd = 40 (40, 42, 42, 44, 46, 56, 58, 62) sts rem.

Set sleeve aside while you knit the second one the same way.

Arrange sleeves and body on larger size circular, matching underarms. Pm at each intersection of body and sleeve. The rnd begins just before right sleeve.

With RS facing, color A and smaller size dpn, pick up and knit sts on side of front for the button band. Work 6 rows in k1 p1 ribbing, but on row 2, make 2 (2, 2, 2, 2, 3, 3, 3) buttonholes. Note that buttonhole no. 3 (3, 3, 3, 4, 4, 4, 4) will be worked later on neckband. Evenly space buttonholes accordingly. *Buttonhole:* BO 2 sts and CO 2 new sts over gap on next row. After completing ribbing rows, BO in ribbing. Make another band the same way on other side of front.

Now work ribbed neckband. With RS facing, color A and smaller size needles, pick up and knit 5 sts on short end of one buttonhole band, knit sts from holder and pick up and knit 5 sts on end of next buttonhole band. Work 6 rows in k1, p1 ribbing, but, on row 2, make a buttonhole on each side: 3 sts ribbing, BO 2 sts, work in ribbing until 5 sts rem, BO 2 sts, 3 sts ribbing. On next row, CO 2 sts over each gap.

BACK (with sleeve stitches)
Working back and forth (the 1st row = WS), continue in stripe pattern.
On every RS row, decrease at raglan markers as before, and, on each end as on front. When you've decreased for raglan a total of 15 (15, 16, 17, 18, 19, 21, 25, 27) times, place sts on a holder. Make button bands as for front (omitting buttonholes). Finally, work neckband in ribbing as on front, but without buttonholes on each side.

FINISHING
Seam underarms. Sew down button bands on yoke on lower ends.
Weave in all ends neatly on WS.
Sew on buttons.
Block by covering T-shirt with a damp towel, leave until completely dry or gently steam-press under a damp pressing cloth.

Knit 2 rnds, continuing in stripe pattern. On next rnd, begin raglan decreases as follows:

K2, sl 1, k1, psso, knit until 4 stst before next marker, k2tog, k2; rep * to * around = 8 sts decreased.

Decrease the same way on every other rnd.
You should have 4 knit sts between decreases at each raglan marker. On the 4th decrease rnd, BO the 4 sts at raglan markers on front and now work front separately.
Place back sts on a holder.

FRONT (continue stripe pattern)
Row 1 (WS): Purl.
Row 2 (RS): Sl 1, k1, psso, knit until 2 sts rem, k2tog.
Rep these 2 rows until you've decreased 11 (11, 12, 13, 14, 15, 17, 21, 23) times [= a total of 15 (15, 16, 17, 18, 19, 21, 25, 27) times] including the decreases before you divided for the front. Place sts on a holder.

From left:

KlompeLompe Tynn merinoull, color 3081, Sandnes Garn
Tynn merinoull, color 7741, Klompleompe Tynn merinoull,
color 2652

Kristoffer Shorts ——————— »

Kristoffer Shorts

Basic shorts to suit everyone.

SIZES: 1 (2, 4, 6, 8, 10) years

FINISHED MEASUREMENTS:
Waist: Approx. 21¾ (22½, 23¼, 24½, 25, 25) in [55.5 (57, 59, 62, 63.5, 63.5) cm]
Length: Approx. 11¾ (13½, 15, 16¼, 17¼, 18½) in [30 (34, 38, 41, 44, 47) cm]

MATERIALS

YARN: Sandnes Garn KlompeLompe Tynn merinoull (fine merino wool) [CYCA #1—fingering, 100% merino wool, 191 yd (175 m) / 50 g]

YARN COLORS AND AMOUNTS:
Gray-Brown 2652: 100 (150, 150, 200, 250, 250) g

NEEDLES: US sizes 1.5 and 2.5 (2.5 and 3 mm): short circulars and sets of 5 dpn; 32 in (80 cm) circular for magic loop if preferred

NOTIONS: Waistband elastic, to fit around waist + seam allowance

GAUGE: 27 sts on larger size needles = 4 in (10 cm).

Adjust needle size to obtain correct gauge if necessary.

The shorts are worked top down, in the round on a circular needle.

With smaller size circular, CO 150 (154, 160, 168, 172, 172) sts. Join, being careful not to twist cast-on row; pm for beginning of rnd.

Knit 10 rnds, purl 1 rnd, knit 4 rnds.
On next rnd, make two eyelet holes:
K68 (70, 73, 77, 79, 79), k2tog, yo, k10, yo, sl 1, k1, psso, k68 (70, 73, 77, 79, 79).
Knit 5 rnds.

Change to larger size circular and knit 1 rnd.
Now raise back with short rows:

Raise back with short rows as follows, and, when you come to a yarnover, work it tog with next st.
K10; turn, yo, p20. Turn, yo, knit until 4 sts past last turn. Turn and purl until 4 sts past last turn. Continue the same way until you've turned 4 (5, 5, 6, 6, 6) times on each side. Knit to beginning of rnd.

Continue in stockinette. Pm on each side of the 6 center sts on front and back. When piece measures 4 (4¾, 5½, 6¼, 7, 7½) in [10 (12, 14, 16, 18, 19) cm] from where you changed to larger size needle, begin shaping center panels:
Increase 1 st with M1 on each side of each 6-st center panel on front and back. Increase the same way on every 3rd rnd a total of 5 times = 20 sts increased.
On next rnd, BO the 6-st panels at front and back and begin working each leg separately = 79 (81, 84, 88, 90, 90) sts for each leg.

LEG
Place sts of one leg on larger size dpn and join to work in the round.

Pm for beginning of rnd (or purl first st of each rnd).

Knit around for 1¼ in (3 cm).

Now shape leg: K1, k2tog, knit until 3 sts rem, sl 1, k1, psso, k1.

Decrease the same way every ¾ in (2 cm) a total of 3 (3, 4, 4, 5, 5) times = 73 (75, 76, 80, 80, 80) sts rem.

Continue in stockinette until pants measure 11¾ (13½, 15, 16¼, 17¼, 18½) in [30 (34, 38, 41, 44, 47) cm] from purl foldline.

Purl 10 rnds and BO on last rnd. The purl sts will fold up as an edging.

Make the second leg the same way.

FINISHING

Join the 6-st center front and back panels with Kitchener st (see page 22). Fold down waistband and sew down on back. Insert waistband elastic, seam ends of elastic, and finish sewing down casing.

Fold up leg edgings and sew down along top. Make an I-cord (see klompelompe.no) to thread through waistband casing.

Weave in all ends neatly on WS.

Block by covering T-shirt with a damp towel, leave until completely dry or gently steam-press under a damp pressing cloth.

Little Garter-Stitch Rompers

These rompers are knitted a bit differently. You begin at the side in garter stitch and work the yoke afterward. So fun!
To top it all off, the rompers have ruffled wings.

SIZES: 0-2 (3, 6, 9, 12, 18, 24) months

FINISHED MEASUREMENTS:
Chest: Approx. 17½ (18¼, 19, 20, 21, 21¾, 22½) in [44.5 (46.5, 48, 51, 53, 55.5, 57) cm]
Total length, from bib down: Approx. 15¼ (16¼, 17, 18¾, 19½, 20, 22½) in [38.5 (41, 43, 47.5, 49.5, 51, 57.5) cm]

YARN: Sandnes Garn KlompeLompe Tynn merinoull (fine merino wool) [CYCA #1—fingering, 100% merino wool, 191 yd (175 m) / 50 g]

YARN COLORS AND AMOUNTS:
Soft Purple 4331: 150 (150, 150, 200, 200, 200, 200) g

NEEDLES: US sizes 1.5 and 2. 5 (2.5 and 3 mm): 16 in (40 cm) circulars [or 32 in (80 cm) magic loop circular]

NOTIONS: 7 (7, 7, 8, 8, 8, 8) buttons

GAUGE: 27 sts on larger size needles = 4 in (10 cm).

Adjust needle size to obtain correct gauge if necessary.

KNITTING TIP

When picking up and knitting stitches over garter st, remember that a ridge has 2 rows, = 2 sts on the edge, so you should pick up 2 sts per ridge if the instructions say to pick up 1 st in every stitch.

The rompers begin at the side and are worked back and forth for the body below yoke.

With larger size circular, CO 48 (54, 56, 62, 68, 72, 76) sts. Work back and forth in garter st (= knit all rows) until piece measures 3¼ (4, 4, 4¾, 4¾, 5¼, 5¼) in [8 (10, 10, 12, 12, 13, 13) cm].

Now increase on each RS row: Knit until 1 st rem, M1, k1.

Increase the same way a total of 7 (7, 8, 8, 8, 8, 8) times.

On next RS row, CO 5 sts at end of row and then continue in garter st for 1¾ in (4.5 cm). On next WS row, CO the first 5 sts.
Now begin decreasing on every RS row: Knit until 3 sts rem, k2tog, k1.
Rep the decrease row a total of 7 (7, 8, 8, 8, 8, 8) times.

Work without decreasing for 4 (5½, 5½, 7, 7, 8, 8) in [10 (14, 14, 18, 18, 20, 20) cm].
Now increase on very RS row: Knit until 1 st rem, M1, k1.
Rep the increase row a total of 24 (24, 25, 25, 25, 25, 25) times.
Continue in garter st without increasing for 1¾ in (4.5 cm).

Now begin decreasing on every RS row: Knit until 3 sts rem, k2tog, k1.
Rep the decrease row a total of 24 (24, 25, 25, 25, 25, 25) times.

Work another ¾ (1½, 1½, 2½, 2½, 2¾, 2¾) in [2 (4, 4, 6, 6, 7, 7) cm] in garter st and then BO. Seam sides.

Work the garter st around the legs with smaller size circular.

With RS facing, pick up and knit 96 (108, 108, 120, 120, 126, 126) sts. Join to work in the round.

Decrease Rnd 1: K22 (28, 28, 30, 30, 33, 33), *k2tog*; rep * to * 26 (26, 26, 30, 30, 30, 30) times, k22 (28, 28, 30, 30, 33, 33) = 70 (82, 82, 90, 90, 96, 96) sts rem.

Decrease Rnd 2: K15 (19, 19, 20, 20, 23, 23), *k2tog*; rep * to * 20 (22, 22, 25, 25, 25, 25) times, k15 (19, 19, 20, 20, 23, 23). Knit 3 rnds, binding off on last rnd.
Work around second leg the same way.

Back Button Band with smaller size needles
Pick up and knit sts on end of garter leg edging and on sts between legs (approx. 1 st in each st but skipping every 4th st). Knit 7 rows and BO on last row.

Front Button Band with smaller size needles
Pick up and knit sts on end of garter leg edging and on sts between legs (approx. 1 st in each st but skipping every 4th st). Knit 7 rows and BO on last row, **but**, on row 2, make 4 buttonholes evenly spaced across. Buttonhole: BO 2 sts and CO 2 sts over gap on next row.

YOKE

Begin at back. With larger size circular, pick up and knit approx. 1 st in every other st.
Knit 1 rnd, adjusting st count to 120 (126, 130, 138, 144, 150, 154) sts.

Work around in stockinette for ¾ in (2 cm). From this point on, work back and forth to make opening at back = knit on RS and purl on WS. Continue in stockinette until yoke is 1¼ (1⅜, 1⅜, 1½, 1¾, 2, 2¼) in [3 (3.5, 3.5, 4, 4.5, 5, 5.5) cm] above row where you picked up sts for yoke.

Divide for Body and Armholes
K23 (24, 25, 25, 27, 28, 29) (= left back), k14 (15, 15, 18, 18, 18, 18) and place sts on holder for armhole, k46 (48, 50, 52, 54, 58, 60) (= front), k14 (15, 15, 18, 18, 18, 18) and place sts on holder for armhole, k23 (24, 25, 25, 27, 28, 29) (= right back).

RIGHT BACK
The first row = WS.
Purl 1 row.
Next Row: K1, k2tog, knit to end of row.
Rep these 2 rows a total of 3 (3, 4, 4, 4, 4, 4) times = 20 (21, 21, 21, 23, 24, 25) sts rem.
Continue back and forth in stockinette until back measures 4¼ (4¾, 5¼, 5½, 5¾, 6, 6¼) in [11 (12, 13, 14, 14.5, 15, 16) cm] from row where you picked up sts. On next row (WS), p8 (9, 9, 9, 10, 10, 10) and place sts on holder. P12 (12, 12,12, 13, 14, 15) rem sts for shoulder.

Next Row: Knit until 3 sts rem, k2tog, k1. Purl across next row.
Rep these 2 rows a total of 4 times.
On next row (RS), BO rem sts.

LEFT BACK
The first row = WS.
Purl 1 row.
Next Row: Knit until 3 sts rem, sl 1, k1, psso, k1.
Rep these 2 rows a total of 3 (3, 4, 4, 4, 4, 4) times = 20 (21, 21, 21, 23, 24, 25) sts rem.
Continue back and forth in stockinette until back measures 4¼ (4¾, 5¼, 5½, 5¾, 6, 6¼) in [11 (12, 13, 14, 14.5, 15, 16) cm] from row where you picked up sts. On next row (WS), purl across and then place last 8 (9, 9, 9, 10, 10, 10) sts on holder. Cut yarn and re-attach so you can work the rem 12 (12, 12, 12, 13, 14, 15) sts for shoulder.

Next Row: K1, k2tog, knit to end of row. Purl across next row.
Rep these 2 rows a total of 4 times.
On next row (RS), BO rem sts.

FRONT

The first row = WS.

Purl 1 row.

Next Row: K1, k2tog, knit until 3 sts rem, sl 1, k1, psso, k1.

Rep these 2 rows a total of 4 times.

Continue back and forth in stockinette without decreasing until front measures 3¼ (3½, 4, 4⅛, 4¼, 4½, 4¾) in [8.5 (9, 10, 10.5, 11, 11.5, 12) cm] from row where you picked up sts. On next row (WS), p26 (28, 30, 32, 33, 36, 37) then place those sts on a holder; purl rem 12 (12, 12 12, 13, 14, 15) sts for shoulder.

Next Row: Knit until 3 sts rem, k2tog, k1. Purl across next row.

Rep these 2 rows a total of 4 times.

Work 7 (9, 9, 11, 11, 11, 11) rows in stockinette, binding off on last row.

Place the first 12 (12, 12 12, 13, 14, 15) sts on holder for right shoulder onto larger size needle.

RS Row: K1, k2tog, knit to end of row.

WS Row: Purl across.

Rep these 2 rows a total of 4 times.

Work 7 (9, 9, 11, 11, 11, 11) rows in stockinette, binding off on last row.

Seam shoulders.

Garter Stitch around Armholes

Begin rnd at center of the 14 (15, 15, 18, 18, 18, 18) sts on holder. With smaller size needle, k7 (7, 7, 9, 9, 9, 9), pick up and knit sts around armhole (skip every 4th st); finish with k7 (8, 8, 9, 9, 9, 9). Knit 1 row on WS, knit 1 rnd on RS, knit 1 row on WS. BO knitwise on next row. Edge the other armhole the same way.

Garter Stitch around Neck

With smaller size needle, knit sts of left back from holder, pick up and knit sts along shoulder (1 st in each st, skipping every 4th st), knit held sts of front, pick up and knit sts along other shoulder, knit held sts of right back. Knit 1 row on WS, knit 1 row on RS, knit 1 row on WS. BO knitwise on next row.

BUTTON BAND ON BACK OPENING

The button band is worked in one piece from right to left side. With smaller size needle, pick up and knit 1 st in each st, skipping every 4th st on each side of opening. Knit 1 row on WS. Knit 1 row on RS and, *at the same time*, make 3 (3, 3, 4, 4, 4, 4) buttonholes evenly spaced on left side. Buttonhole: BO 2 sts. On next row, knit on WS and CO 2 sts over each gap. BO knitwise on next row.

WINGS (make one on each side)

NOTE: After each turn, make a yarnover and tighten yarn.

With larger size needles, pick up and knit sts in a straight line from lower edge of stockinette section on front up to lower edge of stockinette on back. For left wing, begin by picking up on front and, for right wing, begin on back. The sts should be picked up and knitted straight along the garter ridge around each armhole. Pick up 1 st in each st on yoke (see photo above).

Knit 2 rows.

K14 (16, 16, 18, 20, 20, 20), continue knitting with an M1 increase after every 6th st until

14 (16, 16, 18, 20, 20, 20) sts rem; turn.

Knit until 5 sts before last turn; turn.

Knit, increasing with M1 after every 7th st until 5 sts rem before last turn; turn.

Knit until 5 sts before last turn; turn.

Knit across.

BO knitwise.

Sew ends of wings to rompers.

FINISHING

Weave in all ends neatly on WS.

Sew on buttons.

Block by covering rompers with a damp towel and leaving garment until completely dry.

Color 7521

Tilda Summer Dress

Our favorite dress!
Fine yarn and a delicate lace pattern with fun bobbles combine with simple shaping to make a dress everyone will like.

SIZES: 2 (4, 6, 8, 10) years

FINISHED MEASUREMENTS:

Chest: Approx. 22¾ (25¼, 25½, 25¾, 28) in [58 (64, 65, 66.5, 71) cm]

Total length, from bib down: Approx. 18½ (19¼, 21¾, 23¾, 24¾) in [47 (49, 55, 60, 63) cm]

YARN: Sandnes Garn KlompeLompe Tynn merinoull (fine merino wool) [CYCA #1—fingering, 100% merino wool, 191 yd (175 m) / 50 g]

YARN COLORS AND AMOUNTS:

Cream 1013: 150 (200, 250, 250, 300) g

NEEDLES: US sizes 1.5 and 2. 5 (2.5 and 3 mm): 16 and 24 in (40 and 60 cm) circulars and sets of 5 dpn

CROCHET HOOK: US size C-2 (2.5 mm)

NOTIONS: 1 button

GAUGE: 27 sts on larger size needles = 4 in (10 cm).

Adjust needle size to obtain correct gauge if necessary.

STITCHES AND TECHNIQUES

Seed Stitch
Row 1: *K1, p1*; rep * to * across.
Subsequent Rows: Work knit over purl and purl over knit.

The dress is worked top down, beginning back and forth before joining in the round.

With smaller size circular, CO 92 (100, 100, 108, 108). Work 6 rows in seed st.
Change to larger size circular.
Knit 1 row, placing markers:
K18 (20, 20, 22, 22), pm, k10 (sleeve sts), pm, k36 (40, 40, 44, 44), pm, k10 (sleeve sts), pm, k18 (20, 20, 22, 22).
Purl 1 row.

Continue in stockinette, increasing at each marker on every RS row:
Knit until 1 st before marker, RLI; RLI on st after marker = 8 sts increased across.

After working 11 (11, 12, 12, 12) increase rows, join to work in the round. Increase on every other rnd.
After working a total of 17 (19, 20, 20, 22) increase rows/rnds, knit next rnd, placing sleeve sts on holders; CO 8 sts for each underarm = 156 (172, 176, 184, 192) sts.

Knit 10 (12, 12, 14, 16) rnds. Purl 1 rnd, knit 1 rnd.

Knit 1 rnd, increasing 4 (4, 8, 0, 8) sts evenly spaced around = 160 (176, 184, 184, 200) sts.

Knit 14 (14, 18, 20, 24) rnds.
Knit 1 rnd, increasing 16 sts evenly spaced around = 176 (192, 200, 200, 216) sts.
Knit 14 (14, 18, 22, 24) rnds.
Knit 1 rnd, increasing 16 sts evenly spaced around = 192 (208, 216, 216, 232) sts.
Knit 14 (14, 18, 22, 24) rnds.

Knit 0 (1, 1, 1, 1) rnd, increasing 16 sts evenly spaced around
= 192 (224, 232, 232, 248) sts.
Knit 0 (4, 8, 10, 10) rnds.

Now work following chart. Work part A 2 (2, 3, 3, 3) times and
then work part B 2 (2, 3, 3, 3) times.

After completing charted rows, BO with I-cord bind-off (see
video at klompelompe.no). CO 3 sts and slip them to left
needle.
K2, k2tog tbl. Slip the 3 sts on right needle to left needle.
Rep * to * until all sts have been bound off. Seam ends of
I-cord.

KNITTING TIP
If you find it too difficult to manage a double yarnover, you can
move one yarnover on this rnd to the beginning of the next
rnd.

SLEEVES (Make both alike)
With larger size circular, knit the 44 (48, 50, 50, 54) held sleeve
sts.
Work back and forth, beginning on RS. Knit until 2 sts rem;
turn. Sl 1, purl until 2 sts rem. Sl 1, knit until 4 sts rem; turn.
Sl 1, purl until 4 sts rem; turn. Sl 1, knit to end of row. Knit 1
row on WS.
Next Row: K15 (17, 18, 18, 20), *k2tog*; rep * to * 7 times,
k15 (17, 18, 18, 20). Knit 3 rows, binding off on last row. Sew
edges of sleeve to dress.

FINISHING
Crochet a button loop on one side of back neck opening: Ch
5, attach to dress with 1 sl st. Sew button opposite loop.
Weave in all ends neatly on WS.
Block by covering dress with a damp towel, leave until completely
dry or gently steam-press under a damp pressing cloth, but
do not press bobbles.

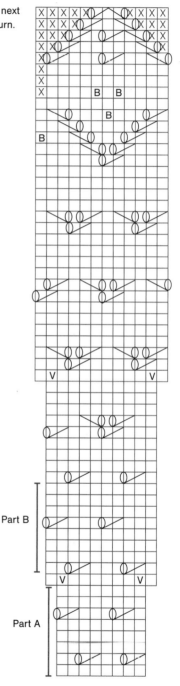

B	Bobble: (K1, yo, k1) in next st; turn. P3; turn. K3; turn. P2tog, p1; turn. K2tog.
	knit
X	purl
	sl 1, k2tog, psso
	k2tog
	sl 1, k1, psso
	1 yo between 2 sts
V	increase here with M1

Part B

Part A

Trixie Pixie Cap

A quick-knit project you can make with or without bobbles.
You can knit it in just one evening!

SIZES: 0-3 (3-6, 6-9 months, 1-2, 3-4 years)

YARN: Sandnes Garn KlompeLompe merinoull [CYCA #3 – DK, light worsted, 100% merino wool, 114 yd (104 m) / 50 g]

YARN COLORS AND AMOUNTS:
Powder Rose 4032: 50 (50, 50, 100, 100) g

NEEDLES: US size 4 (3.5 mm): 16 in (40 cm) circular and set of 5 dpn

GAUGE: 22 sts = 4 in (10 cm).

Adjust needle size to obtain correct gauge if necessary.

STITCHES AND TECHNIQUES

Bobble
(K1, yo, k1) in same st; turn, P3; turn, K3; turn, P3; turn. Sl 2 knitwise as if to knit tog, k1, psso.
Wyf: With yarn held in front

The cap is worked back and forth on two dpn or a short circular.

CO 26 (28, 34, 40, 42) sts.

Work 8 rows stockinette (= knit on RS and purl on WS).
Now work the first 6 (8, 8, 8, 10) sts in garter st (knit on all rows) with rem 20 (20, 26, 32, 32) sts purled with bobbles:

Row 1 (RS): P4, k1, *p5, k1*; rep * to * 2 (2, 3, 4, 4) times, p3.

Row 2: K3, sl 1 purlwise wyf, *k5, sl 1 purlwise wyf*; rep * to * 2 (2, 3, 4, 4) times, k4.

Row 3:
0-3 months: P4, bobble, p5, k1, p5, bobble, p3.
3-6 months: P4, bobble, p5, k1, p5, bobble, p3.
6-9 months: P4, bobble, p5, k1, p5, bobble, p5, k1, p3.
1-2 years: P4, bobble, p5, k1, p5, bobble, p5, k1, p5, bobble, p3.
3-4 years: P4, bobble, p5, k1, p5, bobble, p5, k1, p5, bobble, p3.

Row 4: Work as for Row 2.
Row 5: Work as for Row 1.
Row 6: Work as for Row 3.
Row 7:
0-3 months: P4, k1, p5, bobble, p5, k1, p3.
3-6 months: P4, k1, p5, bobble, p5, k1, p3.
6-9 months: P4, k1, p5, bobble, p5, k1, p5, bobble, p3.
1-2 years: P4, k1, p5, bobble, p5, k1, p5, bobble, k1, p3.
3-4 years: P4, k1, k5, bobble, p5, k1, p5, bobble, p5, k1, p3.

Row 8: Work as for Row 2.

Rep Rows 1-8. If preferred, work them without the bobbles. In that case, rep only Rows 1-2.

Pocket Rompers: Sandnes Garn Duo, color 4344
Blue Cap: KlompeLompe merinoull, color 6521

When you've worked 45 (45, 47, 50, 53) ridges at outer edge and the next row is on RS, finish with 8 rows in stockinette (knit on RS and purl on WS).

Fold cap and seam back. Fold in half the stockinette lower edge and sew down on WS. Make an I-cord (see video at klompelompe.no) to thread through stockinette casing.

I-CORD: Knit all sts, *slide sts to front tip of dpn without turning, bring yarn across back, tugging slightly, and knit sts again. Rep from * until cord is desired length.

FINISHING
Weave in all ends neatly on WS.

Front: color 4344
Center: color 4032
Back: color 1013

Treasure Baby Blanket ——————————— >>

Treasure Baby Blanket

A soft, lovely blanket for your little treasure.
The lace pattern is fun to knit!

FINISHED MEASUREMENTS: Approx. 26½ x 30¾ in (67 x 78 cm)

YARN: Sandnes Garn KlompeLompe merinoull [CYCA #3 – DK, light worsted, 100% merino wool, 114 yd (104 m) / 50 g]

YARN COLORS AND AMOUNTS:

Soft Purple 4331: 350 g

NEEDLES: US size 7 (4.5 mm): 32 in (80 cm) circular

GAUGE: 20 sts = 4 in (10 cm).

Adjust needle size to obtain correct gauge if necessary.

CO 133 sts.
Work 20 rows in seed st:
Row 1: *K1, p1*; rep * to * until 1 st rem, end k1.
Subsequent Rows: Work knit over purl and purl over knit.
Continue with 10 sts in seed st at each side and rem sts in pattern following chart.

Work as est until blanket is approx. 28¾ in (73 cm) long, ending with Row 1 on chart.
Work 20 rows in seed st, binding off in seed st on last row.

FINISHING
Weave in all ends neatly on WS.
Lay a damp towel over blanket and leave until dry.

Part A

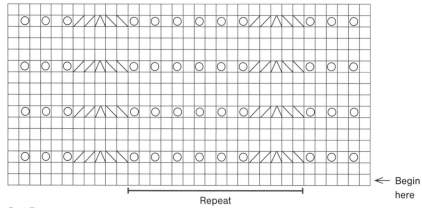

Repeat

← Begin here

Part B

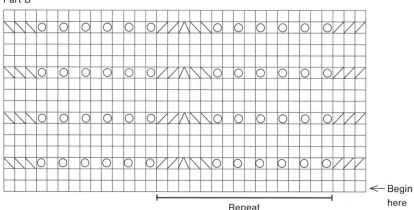

Repeat

← Begin here

Work Part A and then Part B; rep the two charts throughout.

☐ knit on RS, purl on WS

Ⓞ yarnover

� k2tog

◺ sl 1, k1, psso

◸ sl 2 knitwise as if to knit tog, k1, psso

146

Whirligig Cap

A breezy cap for cool summer days.

SIZES: Newborn (1-2, 3-6, 9-12 months, 1-2, 3-6, 8-12 years)

YARN: Sandnes Garn KlompeLompe merinoull [CYCA #3 – DK, light worsted, 100% merino wool, 114 yd (104 m) / 50 g]

YARN COLORS AND AMOUNTS:
Soft Purple 4331: 50 (50, 50, 50, 100, 100, 100) g

NEEDLES: US sizes 4, 6, and 8 (3.5, 4, and 5 mm): 16 in (40 cm) circulars and sets of 5 dpn in 2 smaller sizes

GAUGE: 22 sts on US size 4 (3.5 mm) = 4 in (10 cm).

Adjust needle size to obtain correct gauge if necessary.

With circular US 4 (3.5 mm), CO 60 (66, 72, 80, 88, 88, 88) sts. Join, being careful not to twist cast-on row; pm for beginning of rnd. Work 4 (4, 6, 8, 8, 8, 10) rnds in k1 , p1 ribbing. Change to US 8 (5 mm) circular and knit 1 rnd increasing 5 (4, 3, 10, 7, 12, 22) sts evenly spaced around = 65 (70, 75, 90, 95, 100, 110) sts.

Now work in pattern (wyf = with yarn held in front of work):

NOTE: Do not tighten yarn strands in front of work.
Rnd 1: *K2, sl 3 wyf*; rep * to * around.
Rnd 2: Sl 1 wyf, *k2, sl 3 wyf*; rep * to * until 4 sts rem, k2, sl 2 wyf.

Rnd 3: Sl 2 wyf, *k2, sl 3 wyf*; rep * to * until 3 sts rem, k2, sl 1 wyf.
Rnd 4: Sl 3 wyf, *k2, sl 3 wyf*; rep * to * until 2 sts rem, k2.
Rnd 5: K1, s1 3wyf, *k2, sl 3 wyf*; rep * to * until 1 st rem, k1.
Rep Rnds 1-5 until cap measures 3 (3½, 4¼, 5¼, 5¾, 6½, 7) in [7.5 (9, 11, 13, 14.5, 16.5, 18) cm]. Change to dpn US 6 (4 mm).

Knit 1 rnd, decreasing 5 (0, 5, 10, 5, 10, 20) sts evenly spaced around = 60 (70, 70, 80, 90, 90, 90) sts rem.

SHAPE CROWN
Decrease Rnd 1: *K8, k2tog*; rep * to * around.
Knit 2 rnds.
Decrease Rnd 2: *K7, k2tog*; rep * to * around.
Knit 1 rnd.
Decrease Rnd 3: *K6, k2tog*; rep * to * around.
Knit 1 rnd.
Decrease Rnd 4: *K5, k2tog*; rep * to * around.
Decrease Rnd 5: *K4, k2tog*; rep * to * around.
Decrease Rnd 6: *K3, k2tog*; rep * to * around.

Decrease Rnd 7: *K2, k2tog*; rep * to * around.
Decrease Rnd 8: *K1, k2tog*; rep * to * around.

Cut yarn. Draw end through rem sts and tighten.

Sizes Newborn (1-2, 3-6, 9- 12) months: Make 2 earflaps, spaced 10 sts apart at center back.
With RS facing and US 4 (3.5 mm) dpn, pick up and knit 14 (14, 16, 18) sts. Work 3 rows in stockinette (purl on WS and knit on RS). Now shape earflap by decreasing on every RS row:
RS: K1, sl 1, k1, psso, knit until 3 sts rem, k2tog, k1.
WS: Purl.

Rep these 2 rows until 4 sts rem. On next RS row, K1, k2tog, k1.
Use rem 3 sts to knit an I-cord

I-CORD (see video at klompelompe. no)
K3, *slide sts to front tip of dpn without turning, bring yarn across back, tugging slightly, and knit sts again. Rep from * until cord is approx. 8 in (20 cm) long.

Make second earflap the same way.

FINISHING
Weave in all ends neatly on WS.
If desired, crochet a flower with button to attach to cap.
Lay a damp towel over cap and leave until dry.

CROCHETED FLOWER
with BUTTON

YARN: Your choice
YARN AMOUNT: 50 g or leftovers
1 BUTTON: ¾ in (20 mm) in diameter or your choice
CROCHET HOOK: Size to suit chosen yarn

ABBREVIATIONS
St = stitch(es)
Ch = chain st
Dc = double crochet
Tr = treble crochet
Sl st = slip st

Ch 3 and join into a ring with 1 sl st into 1st ch.

Ch 2, work 10 dc around ring.

PETAL RND 1: Work only into front loops. *Ch 2, 2 dc in next st, 2 dc and 1 sl st into next st*; rep * to * around = 5 flower petals.

PETAL RND 2: Work only into back loops (behind the 5 petals). *Ch 2, 2 dc in each st around.

PETAL RND 3: Work only into front loops. *Ch 2, 2 dc in each of next 4 sts, with 1 sl st in 4th st; rep * to * around = 5 flower petals.

PETAL RND 4: Work only into back loops (behind the 5 new petals). *Ch 2, 1 dc and 1 tr in next st, 2 tr in each of next 4 sts, 1 tr, 1 dc, and 1 sl st in next st*; rep * to * around = 5 petals.

Cut yarn and weave in ends neatly on WS. Sew a ¾ in (20 mm) button to center of flower.

David Doll Jacket ⟶

David Doll Jacket

The same heirloom-quality sweater as the David Sweater-Jacket,
perfectly sized for a teddy bear or doll.

SIZES: One size for doll (Baby Born)

YARN: Sandnes Garn KlompeLompe Tynn merinoull (fine merino wool) [CYCA #1—fingering, 100% merino wool, 191 yd (175 m) / 50 g]

YARN COLORS AND AMOUNTS:
Powder Rose 4032: 50 g

NEEDLES: US sizes 1.5 and 2. 5 (2.5 and 3 mm): 16 or 24 in (40 or 60 cm) circulars (or magic loop), sets of 5 dpn

NOTIONS: 5 buttons

GAUGE: 27 sts on larger size needles = 4 in (10 cm).

Adjust needle size to obtain correct gauge if necessary.

The sweater is worked from the top down, back and forth on a circular needle.

With smaller size circular, CO 61 sts. Work back and forth in k1, p1 ribbing for 6 rows, **but**, on the 3rd row, make a buttonhole: Work 3 sts ribbing, BO 2 sts, rib to end of row. On next row, CO 2 sts over gap. On the buttonhole band, make a total of 5 buttonholes evenly spaced about 1⅜ in (3.5 cm) apart.

NOTE: From this point on, the outermost 5 sts on each side are always knitted on every row for the buttonhole/button bands. *Don't forget to make the buttonholes!*

Change to larger size circular. Knit 1 row, increasing 20 sts evenly spaced across, excluding bands = 81 sts.

Work 4 rows in stockinette.

Knit 3 rows (= knit on WS, knit on RS, knit on WS).
Work 2 rows in stockinette (= knit on RS, purl on WS).
Next Row (RS): Knit 1 row, increasing 20 sts evenly spaced across, excluding bands = 101 sts.
Work 4 rows in stockinette.

Knit 3 rows (= knit on WS, knit on RS, knit on WS).
Work 2 rows in stockinette (= knit on RS, purl on WS).
Next Row (RS): Knit 1 row, increasing 24 sts evenly spaced across, excluding bands = 125 sts.
Work 4 rows in stockinette.

Knit 3 rows (= knit on WS, knit on RS, knit on WS).
Work 2 rows in stockinette (= knit on RS, purl on WS).
Next Row (RS): Knit 1 row, increasing 24 sts evenly spaced across, excluding bands = 149 sts.
Purl 1 row on WS.

On next row, divide for body and sleeves:
K23, place 33 sts on a holder for sleeve, CO 5 new sts for underarm, k37,
place 33 sts on a holder for sleeve, CO 5 new sts for underarm, k23.
Work 2 rows in stockinette.

Continue textured stripe pattern:
Knit 3 rows (= knit on WS, knit on RS, knit on WS).
Work 7 rows in stockinette (= knit on RS, purl on WS).
Rep these 10 rows until body measures 5½ in (14 cm).

Change to smaller size circular and work 8 rows in k1, p1 ribbing. BO on last row.

SLEEVES (make both alike)

With larger size dpn, beginning in center st of the 5 sts cast-on for underarm, pick up and knit 3 sts, k33 held sleeve sts, pick up and knit 2 sts on underarm.

KNITTING TIP

If you have trouble picking up and knitting stitches, you can cast on new sts and later join them with Kitchener stitch (see page 22).

Join to work in the round. The first st is a marked st (pm around st) and always purled.
Knit 2 rnds.

Now work around in textured stripe pattern: Purl 1 rnd, knit 1 rnd, purl 1 rnd, knit 7 rnds.
Rep these 10 rnds for sleeve.

After 1 in (2.5 cm), decrease 1 st on each side of marked st. Decrease the same way every ¾ in (2 cm) until 32 sts rem and sleeve is 3¼ in (8 cm) long.
Change to smaller size dpn and work 8 rnds in k1, p1 ribbing. BO in ribbing on last rnd.

FINISHING

Seam underarms. Sew on buttons. Weave in all ends neatly on WS.
Block by covering sweater with a damp towel and leaving it until completely dry.

David Doll Rompers

Mini rompers to fit a doll. Once you've made one, we guarantee,
you'll want to make more!

SIZES: One size for doll (Baby Born)

YARN: Sandnes Garn KlompeLompe Tynn merinoull (fine merino wool) [CYCA #1—fingering, 100% merino wool, 191 yd (175 m) / 50 g]

YARN COLORS AND AMOUNTS:
Gray-Brown 2652 or XX 2024: 50 g

NEEDLES: US sizes 1.5 and 2. 5 (2.5 and 3 mm): 16 or 24 in (40 or 60 cm) circulars (or magic loop), sets of 5 dpn

NOTIONS: 2 buttons

GAUGE: 27 sts on larger size needles = 4 in (10 cm).

Adjust needle size to obtain correct gauge if necessary.

The rompers begin with the bib at the top and are initially worked back and forth.

With smaller size circular, CO 31 sts. Beginning on RS, work 6 rows in k1, p1 ribbing, but, on 3rd row, make 2 buttonholes: 3 sts ribbing, BO 2 sts, continue in ribbing until 5 sts rem, BO 2 sts, work 3 sts in ribbing. On next row, CO 2 sts over each gap.

Change to larger size circular. Now work the outermost 4 sts at each side in garter st (= knit on all rows), and rem sts in 10-row textured stripe pattern = 7 rows stockinette, knit 1 row on WS, knit 1 row on RS, knit 1 row on WS.

Work in pattern as est until piece measures 2½ in (6.5 cm). Cut yarn.

CO 30 sts, work the 31 sts already on needle as est, CO 29 sts = 90 sts. The first st is at center back—join and pm for beginning of rnd.

Now work 6 rnds in ribbing on the new sts you cast on + the 4 previously worked garter sts at each side. Rem sts are worked in textured stripe pattern.

Raise back with short rows as follows:
K16; turn, yo, p31. Turn, yo, k39. Turn, yo, p47. Turn, yo. Knit to end of rnd. **NOTE:** When you come to a yarnover, work yarnover and next st tog.

Continue, working in textured stripe pattern on all sts around and in row sequence from bib.

TEXTURED STRIPE PATTERN IN THE ROUND:
Knit 7 rnds, purl 1 rnd, knit 1 rnd, purl 1 rnd.

When piece measures 5½ in (14 cm), cut yarn and slip next 21 sts to right needle.

Work the back 40 sts (back) back and forth in textured stripe pattern.

On next RS row, k2tog, work until 2 sts rem, k2tog.

Decrease the same way on every RS row until 20 sts rem.

Place the 13 sts at each side onto holders and work the 24 sts at center front in textured stripe pattern. On next RS row, k2tog, work until 2 sts rem, k2tog. Decrease the same way on every RS row until 20 sts rem.

Continue in pattern without decreasing until front is approx. ⅜ in (1 cm) shorter than back. BO.

Join front and back with Kitchener st (see page 22).

With smaller size dpn, pick up and knit about 3 sts for every 4 sts around one leg, knit sts from holder. Divide sts onto 4 dpn and join.

Work 4 rnds in k1, p1 ribbing, binding off in ribbing on last rnd.

STRAPS

With smaller size needle, pick up and knit 19 sts at center back on ribbing. Work 8 rows in k1, p1 ribbing. On next row, BO center st and work each 9-st strap separately.

Work in k1, p1 ribbing until strap measures 5¼ in (13 cm) from row where you picked up sts. BO and work second strap the same way.

FINISHING

Weave in all ends neatly on WS.
Sew on a button at end of each strap.
Block by covering rompers with a damp towel and leaving garment until completely dry.

Tulla Doll Skirt

If you have a little yarn left over from the Tulla skirt,
you can make a matching skirt for a doll.

〰〰〰〰〰〰〰〰〰〰

SIZES: One size for doll (Baby Born)
YARN: Sandnes Garn KlompeLompe Tynn merinoull (fine merino wool) [CYCA #1—fingering, 100% merino wool, 191 yd (175 m) / 50 g]
YARN COLORS AND AMOUNTS:
Blue-Green 6571: 50 g
NEEDLES: US size 2. 5 (3 mm): 16 and 24 in (40 and 60 cm) circulars
NOTIONS: Waistband elastic—to fit around waist + seam allowance
GAUGE: 27 sts = 4 in (10 cm).
Adjust needle size to obtain correct gauge if necessary.

STITCHES AND TECHNIQUES

Elongated knit stitch (ek): Knit 1 between the k2tog and 1 slipped st 2 rounds below, k1, pulling loop up with right needle tip to elongate it. Work the next ek in same hole. See video at klompelompe.no.

The skirt is worked bottom up in the round on a circular needle.

SKIRT

CO 120 sts. Join, being careful not to twist cast-on row; pm for beginning of rnd.

Work 4 rnds in seed st (Rnd 1 = k1, p1; on subsequent rnds, work purl over knit and knit over purl). Knit 2 rnds.

PATTERN

Rnd 1: *K2tog, sl 1, k1, psso, k4*; rep * to * around.
Rnd 2: Knit around.
Rnd 3: *1 ek, k2, 1 ek, 4*; rep * to * around.
Rnd 4: Knit around.
Rnd 5: *K4, k2tog, sl 1, k1, psso*; rep * to * around.
Rnd 6: Knit around.
Rnd 7: *K4, 1 ek, k2, 1 ek*; rep * to * around.
Rnd 8: Knit around.

Repeat Rnds 1-8 of pattern until skirt measures approx. 2½ in (6 cm).
Knit 2 rnds, purl 1 rnd.
Decrease Rnd 1: *K6, k2tog*; rep * to * around = 105 sts rem.

Work 9 rnds in stockinette

Decrease Rnd 2: *K5, k2tog*; rep * to * around = 90 sts rem.

Work 7 rnds in stockinette

Butterfly Cardigan: color A: 6521,
color B 1013, color C: 7251, color
D: 6571

Tulla Skirt and Tulla Doll Skirt:
color 6571

David Doll Jacket: color 6521

Decrease Rnd 3: *K4, k2tog*; rep * to * around = 75 sts rem.
Knit 1 rnd.

Work 8 rnds in seed st.
Purl 1 rnd (foldline) and then work 7 rnds in stockinette.
BO, making sure bind-off is not too tight.

FINISHING

Fold waist facing to WS and sew down, leaving an opening for elastic. Insert elastic and seam short ends of elastic; finish closing casing. Weave in all ends neatly on WS. Block by gently steam-pressing skirt under a damp pressing cloth.

Blueberry Girl's Doll Kerchief

Quickly knit even though it's on fine needles. The doll's mother must, of course, also have a kerchief (see page 64).

(see page 64)

SIZES: One size for doll (Baby Born)

YARN: Sandnes Garn KlompeLompe Tynn merinoull (fine merino wool) [CYCA #1—fingering, 100% merino wool, 191 yd (175 m) / 50 g]

YARN COLORS AND AMOUNTS:
Powder Pink 4344: 50 g

NEEDLES: US size 1.5 and 2. 5 (2.5 and 3 mm): 16 or 24 in (40 or 60 cm) circulars

GAUGE: 27 sts = 4 in (10 cm).
Adjust needle size to obtain correct gauge if necessary.

With smaller size circular, CO 61 sts. Work 8 rows in stockinette (= knit on RS and purl on WS); the 1st row = RS.
Next Row (picot foldline): *K2tog, yo*; rep * to * across, ending with k1.
Work 9 rows in stockinette.

Change to larger size needle.
Work 8 rows in stockinette.
Lace Row 1: K9, k2tog, yo, *k8, k2tog, yo*; rep * to * across until 10 sts rem, k10.
Work 9 rows in stockinette.

Lace Row 2: K4, k2tog, yo, *k8, k2tog, yo*; rep * to * across until 5 sts rem, k5.

Now work a lace row on every 10th row, staggering lace holes as above.
Work 3 rows stockinette (with lace if in pattern).

Now continue in stockinette and lace, but add side bands (work the outermost 5 sts at each side in seed st: k1, p1 on first row and work purl over knit and knit over purl on subsequent rows) and decrease: Work 5 seed sts, k2tog, stockinette (with lace as est) until 7 sts rem, sl 1, k1, psso, 5 seed sts. Rep the decreases on every RS row, continuing lace pattern.

When 3 sts rem between the seed st bands and you are on a RS row, work Kerchief Tip Rows:

Row 1: 5 seed sts, sl 1, k2tog, psso, 5 seed sts.
Row 2: 5 seed sts, p1, 5 seed sts.
Row 3: 4 seed sts, sl 1, k2tog, psso, 4 seed sts.
Row 4: 9 seed sts.
Row 5: 3 seed sts, sl 1 purlwise, p2tog, psso, 3 seed sts.
Row 6: 7 seed sts.
Row 7: 2 seed sts, sl 1, k2tog, psso, 2 seed sts.
Row 8: 5 seed sts.
Row 9: 1 seed st, sl 1 purlwise, p2tog, psso, 1 seed st.
Row 10: Sl 1 purlwise, p2tog, psso.

FINISHING

Cut yarn, draw end through rem sts and tighten.
Weave in all ends neatly on WS. Before adding ribbing around neck, gently steam-press kerchief under a damp pressing cloth.

With smaller size needle, pick up and knit 25 sts along one side of neck, CO 9 sts, pick up and knit 25 sts along other side of neck = 59 sts total.

Work 8 rows in k1, p1 ribbing. On last row, BO in ribbing except for the first 4 and last 4 sts. These sts will be used for I-cord ties. On each side of ribbing, use rem 4 sts to knit an I-cord (see below) about 6¼ in (16 cm) long.

Weave in rem ends neatly on WS.

I-CORD: Using dpn, knit across, *slide sts back to front of needle without turning. Knit across, pulling yarn across WS.* Rep * to * until cord is desired length. Cut yarn, draw end through rem sts and tighten.

David Doll Jacket: color 4032 Powder Rose
David Doll Rompers: color 2652 Gray-Brown

Sewn KlompeLompe Flower

With your choice of fabric, cut out 5 or 3 circles. Make the circles any size you want. The flower will be a little larger than the circles you cut out.

Fold each circle in half and sew around edge with long basting stitches. Tighten and bring ends together. After shaping each circle, sew them together. Embellish the flower with a wood button.

The flower makes a nice decoration for caps and sweater-jackets or for a simple headband.

Little Garter-Stitch Rompers: color 4331 Soft Purple

Lilly Baby Cap

A delicate summer cap for baby, knitted with our well-known Lilly pattern.

SIZES: newborn (1-3, 6-9 months, 1-2, 3-4 years)

YARN: Sandnes Garn KlompeLompe Tynn merinoull (fine merino wool) [CYCA #1—fingering, 100% merino wool, 191 yd (175 m) / 50 g]

YARN COLORS AND AMOUNTS:
Putty 1013: 50 (50, 50, 50, 50) g

NEEDLES: US sizes 1.5 and 2.5 (2.5, and 3 mm): 16 in (40 cm) circulars and sets of 5 dpn

GAUGE: 27 sts on US size 4 (3.5 mm) = 4 in (10 cm).

Adjust needle size to obtain correct gauge If necessary.

The cap begins with the leaf panel.

With larger size circular, CO 21 sts. Work following chart. After rep charted rows 12 (13, 14, 15, 16) times, BO. Steam-press strip well under a damp pressing cloth before you continue. Sew the ends together on pattern row.

With smaller size circular, pick up and knit 84 (92, 98, 102, 110) sts along lower edge of panel, about 1 st for every 7 out of 8 sts. Join and work 7 rnds k2, p2 ribbing.

Next Rnd: Continue ribbing as est, decreasing as follows: BO 8 (9, 10, 11, 12) sts, work next 16 (18, 20, 20, 22) sts and slip them to a holder, BO 36 (38, 38, 40, 42) sts, work next 16 (18, 20, 20, 22) sts and slip them to a holder, BO 8 (9, 10, 11, 12) sts.

Work over each set of 16 (18, 20, 20, 22) sts for an earflap: Begin on RS. Work 4 rows in stockinette (knit on RS and purl on WS). Now begin decreasing on every RS row as follows: K1, sl 1, k1, psso, knit until 3 sts rem, k2tog, k1.
Continue as est until 4 sts rem.

Use rem 4 sts for I-cord tie 7 in (18 cm) long.

I-CORD: Using dpn, knit across, *slide sts back to front of needle without turning. Knit across, pulling yarn across WS.* Rep * to * until cord is long. Cut yarn, draw end through rem sts and tighten.

Make the second earflap the same way.

With larger size circular, pick up and knit 84 (92, 98, 102, 110) sts along top edge of lace panel, with about 1 st for every 7 out of 8 sts = approx. 7 sts per repeat.

Join and knit 4 (6, 10, 14,16) rnds.
Knit 1 rnd, decreasing 4 (4, 2, 6, 6) sts evenly spaced around
= 80 (88, 96, 96, 104) sts rem.

SHAPE CROWN

Decrease Rnd 1: *K6, k2tog*; rep * to * around.
Knit 2 rnds.
Decrease Rnd 2: *K5, k2tog*; rep * to * around.
Knit 2 rnds.
Decrease Rnd 3: *K4, k2tog*; rep * to * around.
Knit 2 rnds.
Decrease Rnd 4: *K3, k2tog*; rep * to * around.

Decrease Rnd 5: *K6, k2tog*; rep * to * around, ending with
k 0 (4, 0, 0, 4).
Decrease Rnd 6: *K5, k2tog*; rep * to * around, ending with
k 0 (4, 0, 0, 4).
Decrease Rnd 7: *K4, k2tog*; rep * to * around, ending with
k 0 (4, 0, 0, 4).
Decrease Rnd 8: *K3, k2tog*; rep * to * around, ending with
k 0 (4, 0, 0, 4).
Decrease Rnd 9: *K2, k2tog*; rep * to * around.
Decrease Rnd 10: *K2tog*; rep * to * around, ending with
k1 (0, 0, 0, 0).

Cut yarn. Draw end through rem sts and tighten.

FINISHING

Weave in all ends neatly on WS.
Gently steam-press cap under a damp pressing cloth.

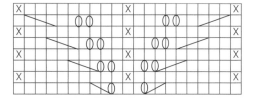

	knit on RS, purl on WS
X	purl on RS, knit on WS
	k2tog
	sl 1 knitwise, k1, psso
	k3tog
	sl 2 knitwise as if to knit tog, k1, psso
	yarnover between 2 sts

Index

ACCESSORIES

Sewn KlompeLompe
   flower   162
Treasure baby blanket   148

DOLL CLOTHES

Blueberry girl kerchief   160
David doll jacket   152
David doll rompers   154
Tulla doll skirt   156

PANTS

Billie shorts   52
David rompers   24
Kangaroo pants   12
Kristoffer shorts   126
Lace tights   92
Little garter-stitch
   rompers   128
Olivia summer onesie   8
Pocket rompers   86

**SKIRTS, DRESSES, AND
TUNICS**

Pocket dress   56
Tilda dress-leotard   100
Tilda summer dress   136
Tulla skirt   17
Vaja tunic   106

SOCKS, CAPS, AND SCARVES

Billie cap   49
Blueberry girl's summer
   kerchief   64
Butterfly cap   36
Butterfly headband   41
Crowberry cap   114
David cap   31
David socks   28
Dinosaur cap   80
Dinosaur headband   84
Lilly baby cap   164
Little Deer bonnet   96
Trixie Pixie cap   140
Whirligig cap   148

SWEATERS

Gurine vest   64
Henry pullover   110
Theodor T-shirt   122

SWEATER-JACKETS

Butterfly cardigan   32
David sweater-jacket   20
Dinosaur cardigan   74
Eivind jacket   44
Spinnvill hooded jacket   60
Wing sweater-jacket   117

Acknowledgments

Once more, we thank our superb test knitters, who organized and went through the pattern instructions for us. They are invaluable to us.

TEST KNITTERS: Britt Alise Kvalevaag Stange, Vera Djapic Oosterkamp, Marianne Hartwedt, Johanna F. K. Gismervik, Ingrid Haavikbotn Hiller, Astrid Apeland Thorsen, Liv Gismervik, Gunn Nordis R. Ekornrud, Ingebjørg Thorsen, Aina Pedersen, Mary Therese Utvik, Ingrid Gudmundsen, Gunn Marit Hølland, Sissel Eikeland, Ida Helland, Gunnvor Thulin, Tove Kalstø Milje, Ingrid J. D. Bergland, Svanhild Andreassen, Tina Kvilhaug, Rakel Bergjord, Linda Andreassen, Kristine Høvring, Vibeke E. Lindtner, Mette Brinchmann, Berthe Rossabø, Åse Elise Osmundsen, Aina Kristin Størkersen, Nancy Hetland, Line Fossberg Taranger, Eli Helgeland Qvale, Randi Andreassen, Caroline Lillesund, Katherine Hettervik, Rhonda H. Nes, Gro Torunn Utvik, Ragnhild Omvik, Silje Kristin Berge, Eva Britt Kvalevaag, Hege B. Hamre, and Karen Qvale.

Many, many thanks to all our models, who made the book so very fine.

MODELS: Olivia, Ludvig, Tiril, David Å., David T., Jostein, Markus, Henry, Elina, Selma, Tora, Nora Martine, Einar, Gina-Elise, Helene, Tilda, Theodor, Lydia, Thor Elias, Atlas, Sarah, Kristoffer, Anna Elise, Tilje, Tuva, and Tora Marthea.

We also want to give a big thanks to Sandnes Garn for such a great collaboration.

We had the world's best publisher at our backs. Thank you for all the work you did and your unstinting enthusiasm.

We owe a big thank-you to our steadfast book designer, Anne Vines.